SharePoint™ User's Guide

Other Microsoft Windows resources from O'Reilly

Related titles

Windows XP Pro: The Missing Manual

Windows XP Home: The Missing Manual

Windows XP in a Nutshell

Learning Windows Server 2003

Windows Server Cookbook

Windows Books Resource Center

windows.oreilly.com is a complete catalog of O'Reilly's Windows and Office books, including sample chapters and code examples.

oreillynet.com is the essential portal for developers interested in open and emerging technologies, including new platforms, programming languages, and operating systems.

Conferences

O'Reilly brings diverse innovators together to nurture the ideas that spark revolutionary industries. We specialize in documenting the latest tools and systems, translating the innovator's knowledge into useful skills for those in the trenches. Visit *conferences.oreilly.com* for our upcoming events.

Safari Bookshelf (*safari.oreilly.com*) is the premier online reference library for programmers and IT professionals. Conduct searches across more than 1,000 books. Subscribers can zero in on answers to time-critical questions in a matter of seconds. Read the books on your Bookshelf from cover to cover or simply flip to the page you need. Try it today with a free trial.

SharePoint™ User's Guide

Infusion Development Corporation

Bryan Acker, Tyler Davey, and Robert McGovern

O'REILLY®

Beijing · Cambridge · Farnham · Köln · Paris · Sebastopol · Taipei · Tokyo

SharePoint™ User's Guide
by Infusion Development Corporation

Published by O'Reilly Media, Inc., 1005 Gravenstein Highway North, Sebastopol, CA 95472.

O'Reilly books may be purchased for educational, business, or sales promotional use. Online editions are also available for most titles (*safari.oreilly.com*). For more information, contact our corporate/institutional sales department: (800) 998-9938 or *corporate@oreilly.com*.

Contributing Writers: Bryan Acker, Tyler Davey, and Robert McGovern

Editor: John Osborn

Production Editor: Matt Hutchinson

Production Services: GEX, Inc.

Cover Designer: Ellie Volckhausen

Interior Designer: David Futato

Printing History:

March 2005: First Edition.

This book uses RepKover™, a durable and flexible lay-flat binding.

ISBN: 0-596-00908-9

[M]

Table of Contents

Preface

Today's business environment requires fast, efficient, and effective communication between employees. Windows SharePoint™ Services provides you with a web-based mechanism for enabling and encouraging communication by allowing you to quickly create web sites (or portals) where you and your team can work together.

For example, using Windows SharePoint Services, you can create a web site that describes a corporate meeting and lists the names of the meeting moderator and attendees, as well as providing the following features:

- A tool for inviting attendees and confirming attendance
- A list displaying the agenda for the meeting
- A set of directions (and possibly a map) showing how to get to the meeting
- A place to store meeting notes
- A way to list and assign tasks generated by the meeting

The best part is that all you have to do is decide which of these features you want on your meeting site. Windows SharePoint Services takes care of generating all the code needed to build the site and then renders it automatically. All you have to provide are the meeting details.

Perhaps you need to create a team collaboration site for a committee charged with deciding the best practices of your company. Windows SharePoint Services gives you the tools you need to build a team site that contains:

- A document library for storing all drafts of your best-practices document
- A discussion board for collecting questions and comments
- A notice board for announcing when the next draft of a document will be released

You can also control the security on your site so that anyone can view the draft documents, but only committee members can make changes. Once again, Windows SharePoint Services provides all the functionality, and all you need to provide are the site layout, content, and security settings.

Who This Book Is For

This is a book for SharePoint users that shows you how to perform the most common Windows SharePoint Services tasks. If you are a newcomer to Windows SharePoint Services, you can read the book from cover to cover. You can also open the book to the section that describes the task you need to perform and follow the step-by-step procedures provided.

Windows SharePoint Services is a set of tools that can be used by anyone. However, in order to use SharePoint effectively, you should have a basic understanding of Microsoft applications, including Office. For certain features of Windows SharePoint Services, you may need to be familiar with basic web page terminology. If you are going to develop your own site, you may also need some experience with HTML design and Microsoft FrontPage.

About This Book

This book provides step-by-step instruction on how to perform the most common tasks you'll encounter in putting Windows SharePoint Services to work for you and your business. Each of the chapters in this book will help you learn some of the basic functionality that can be incorporated into a team site.

Chapter 1, *Working with Sites and Workspaces*, introduces you to the SharePoint environment and terminology. The purpose of Chapter 1 is to familiarize you with the topics that are presented in greater detail in subsequent chapters

Chapter 2, *Basic Web Parts*, outlines the standard built-in Web Parts and their functionality. It also explains how to manage site permissions and versioning control and how these features can be applied to a team site.

Although the standard Web Parts allow you to build an extensive team site, you may require additional functionality. Chapter 3, *Extending Site Pages*, introduces the topics of linking external content, using connectable Web Parts, and creating custom Web Parts. Note that although these topics are introduced, actually creating custom Web Parts is beyond the scope of this book.

Adding content to your site is only part of building an effective Windows SharePoint Services solution. You must secure your team site and libraries to ensure users can only view the information they are supposed to see. Chapter 4, *Securing SharePoint Sites*, introduces the topics of user and site group management, security architecture, and how to assign roles to groups and objects.

SharePoint Services can be integrated with Microsoft Office 2003 to add even more functionality to your team site. Chapter 5, *Integrating with Office 2003*, details the steps to configure your team site to determine online presence. By using online presence, you can send team members real-time messages, as well as set meetings and appointments. SharePoint Services allows team members to work collaboratively on documents in shared workspaces.

Although most end users will not be required to deploy SharePoint Services, Chapter 6, *Setting Up Windows SharePoint Services*, outlines the software and hardware requirements required to deploy SharePoint Services. Chapter 6 also details the required steps to install SharePoint Services and integrate SharePoint Services with SharePoint Portal Server 2003.

Now that you know what this book is about, we should explain what this book is *not* about. This book is not a developer's guide or a complete reference guide. The topics presented are intended for inexperienced users. The material is not intended for people already familiar with all aspects of the SharePoint Services environment.

Conventions Used in This Book

The following typographical conventions are used in this book:

Plain text
: Indicates menu titles, menu options, menu buttons, and keyboard accelerators (such as Alt and Ctrl)

Italic
: Indicates new terms, URLs, email addresses, filenames, file extensions, pathnames, and directories

`Constant width`
: Indicates commands, options, switches, variables, attributes, keys, XML tags, HTML tags, macros, the contents of files, or the output from commands

`Constant width bold`
: Shows commands or other text that should be typed literally by the user

This icon signifies a tip, suggestion, or general note.

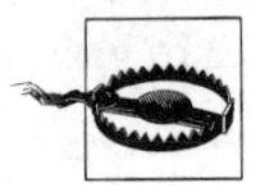

This icon indicates a warning or caution.

We at O'Reilly appreciate, but do not require, attribution. An attribution usually includes the title, author, publisher, and ISBN. For example: "*SharePoint User's Guide* by Infusion Development Corporation. Copyright 2005 O'Reilly Media, Inc., 0-596-00908-9."

If you feel your use of code examples falls outside fair use or the permission given above, feel free to contact us at *permissions@oreilly.com*.

We'd Like to Hear from You

Please address comments and questions concerning this book to the publisher:

O'Reilly Media, Inc.
1005 Gravenstein Highway North
Sebastopol, CA 95472
(800) 998-9938 (in the United States or Canada)
(707) 829-0515 (international or local)
(707) 829-0104 (fax)

We have a web page for this book, where we list errata, examples, and any additional information. You can access this page at:

http://www.oreilly.com/catalog/sharepoint/

To comment or ask technical questions about this book, send email to:

bookquestions@oreilly.com

For more information about O'Reilly books, conferences, Resource Centers, and the O'Reilly Network, see the web site at:

http://www.oreilly.com

When you see a Safari® Enabled icon on the cover of your favorite technology book, that means the book is available online through the O'Reilly Network Safari Bookshelf.

Safari offers a solution that's better than e-books. It's a virtual library that lets you easily search thousands of top tech books, cut and paste code samples, download chapters, and find quick answers when you need the most accurate, current information. Try it for free at *http://safari.oreilly.com*.

CHAPTER 1

Working with Sites and Workspaces

To understand the power of Windows SharePoint Services, you must first understand how SharePoint sites organize and access content. A *SharePoint site* is a web site that creates the base structure for everything you do with Windows SharePoint Services. SharePoint sites provide you with the ability to collaborate on documents, facilitate a meeting, and organize your team's content and ideas.

In this chapter, you will learn about:

- The types of sites SharePoint supports
- How to access, browse, and search a SharePoint site
- How to create and edit a SharePoint site
- How to personalize a SharePoint site

After reading this chapter, you should have a strong understanding of managing and working with SharePoint sites.

Types of SharePoint Sites

Windows SharePoint Services gives you the ability to create sites for both internal and external use. Within the context of Windows SharePoint Services, a *site* can be either a *team site* or a *workspace*. Team sites provide users with a place where they can collaborate on projects. Workspaces are designed to facilitate more specific tasks, such as reviewing documents or planning a meeting.

Team Site

A basic SharePoint site is known as a team site. When you install SharePoint, a default top-level team site is automatically created. This first team site provides you with a starting point for creating additional team sites or workspaces.

A basic team site incorporates many individual collaboration tools, or *Web Parts*, including:

Lists
: Lists form the heart of a SharePoint site and can be used for many things, from storing documents to creating alerts to creating discussions and surveys.

Document libraries
: Document libraries let you store documents in a SharePoint site. You can apply access rights to grant or deny users access to specific document libraries. Also, you can use version control to document each change a user makes to a document.

Picture libraries
: Picture libraries allow you to store, manipulate, and control image files in many formats, including *.bmp*, *.gif*, and *.jpg*.

Discussions
: A SharePoint discussion is a built-in message board that allows the team to discuss issues in an interactive way.

Surveys
: A survey is an interactive form that allows team members to provide feedback in an organized fashion.

Every item in this list is a Web Part. Web Parts are reusable components that you can add to team sites and workspaces. Web Parts provide most of the functionality within any SharePoint site. Web Parts are discussed in Chapters 2 and 3.

A team site increases team productivity by giving team members a central web site for document management, team discussions, surveys, alerts, tasks, and lists. Figure 1-1 displays a typical team site.

Note that the team site is divided into several distinct content zones, allowing for easy navigation and organization. Each content zone contains related elements. For example, the left-most zone is colored blue and contains navigation links, whereas the middle zone contains two Web Parts (Announcements and Events). You can organize your site in the manner that best suits your particular team. Organizing a site and its zones is discussed in the section "Working with SharePoint Sites."

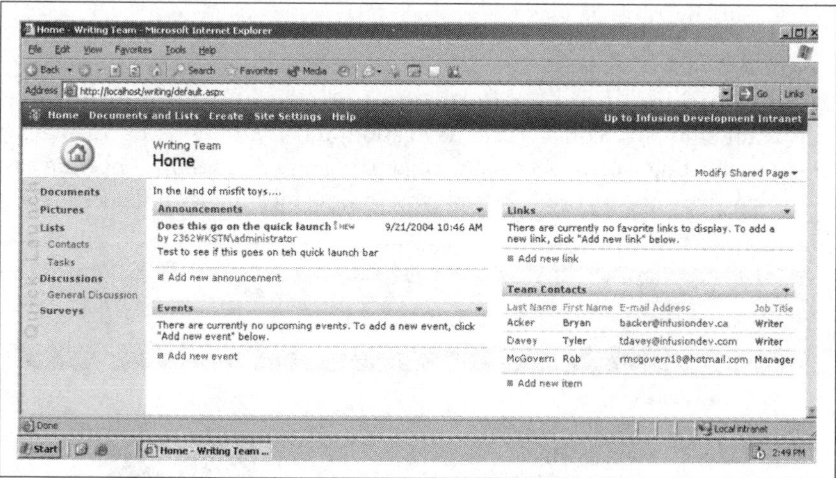

Figure 1-1. A sample team site

Document Workspace

A *document workspace* is a specialized team site designed to facilitate collaboration on shared documents. A document workspace lets you create:

- Lists
- Document libraries
- Discussions
- Surveys

Naturally, you can add any other Web Parts that you might need to the site as well.

Document workspaces look very much like team sites. If the members of your team use Office 2003, they can also access and work with the documents in a document workspace using Office applications such as Excel, Word and PowerPoint. Integrating Office applications with SharePoint is discussed further in Chapter 5.

Meeting Workspace

A meeting workspace is used to create and manage meetings. Meeting workspaces provide users with the ability to:

- Use document libraries
- Display meeting attendees

- Create meeting agendas
- Set meeting objectives

Meeting workspaces use a different structure than document workspaces and team sites. By reducing the navigation and the options for displaying content, meeting workspaces make organizing and discussing a meeting easier for participants. Figure 1-2 displays a sample meeting workspace.

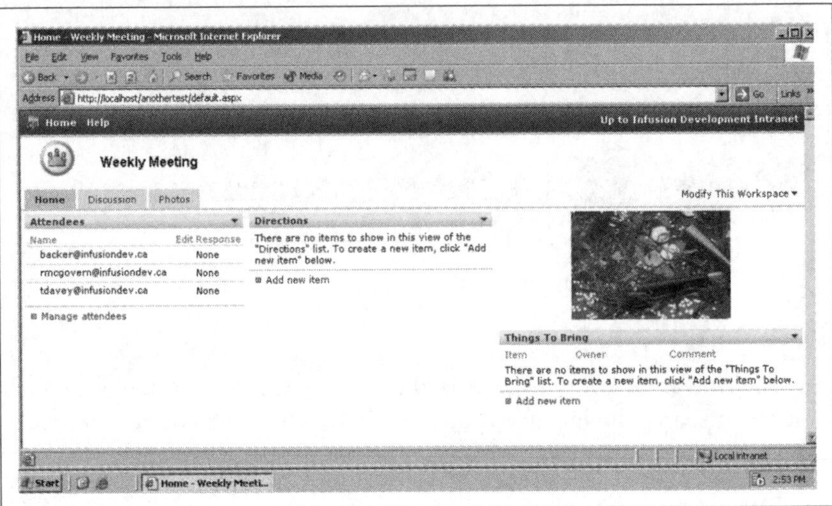

Figure 1-2. A sample meeting workspace

Note that the meeting workspace lacks the left navigation bar and the middle and right content zones found at a team site. Instead, the workspace is designed specifically for presenting information about a meeting, including the attendee list, directions to the meeting, the meeting agenda, a "things to bring" list, and other meeting-specific content.

Working with SharePoint Sites

SharePoint Services helps you locate a site by providing navigation links, a search framework, and standardized site layouts. These features help increase the productivity of your team and other users by reducing the time spent trying to locate a site or master the details of a new site layout.

Locating a Site

In order to work with a SharePoint site, you must first know how to get to it from a web browser. Without knowing its direct link, finding the site can be challenging. SharePoint solves this problem by providing a page that lists all available sites.

Once your system administrator installs SharePoint, he will provide you a URL that points to the SharePoint home page. If you do not know this URL, ask your SharePoint administrator to provide you with the appropriate link.

From the Manage Sites and Workspaces page, you can access:

- Team sites
- Document workspaces
- Meeting workspaces

To access this page:

1. Go to the SharePoint home page and click Documents on the Quick Launch menu or Documents and Lists on the top menu bar.
2. Click the Sites link on the lefthand menu under the See Also section.

If you want to locate a document workspace or meeting workspace, you can click on the associated links in the same section.

3. The current view displays the team sites you can access. If you want to view the document workspaces and meeting workspaces as well, click All under the section Select a View on the lefthand side. To filter just document workspaces or meeting workspaces, you can select the associated links on the lefthand side.

Figure 1-3 shows the list of all sites and workspaces at the Infusion Development intranet site.

Browsing a Site

Once you have found a specific site, you can click the title of the site, which will forward you to the home page. Figure 1-4 displays a typical team site home page, in this case the site used by the writers of this book.

SharePoint separates a site into three distinct navigation areas. While the content in these areas may change, their location will usually remain the same.

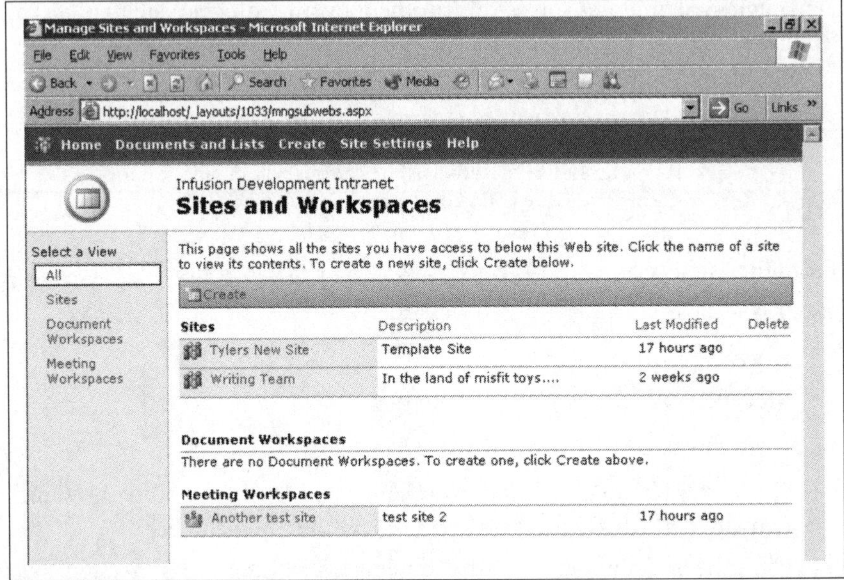

Figure 1-3. Sites and Workspaces main page

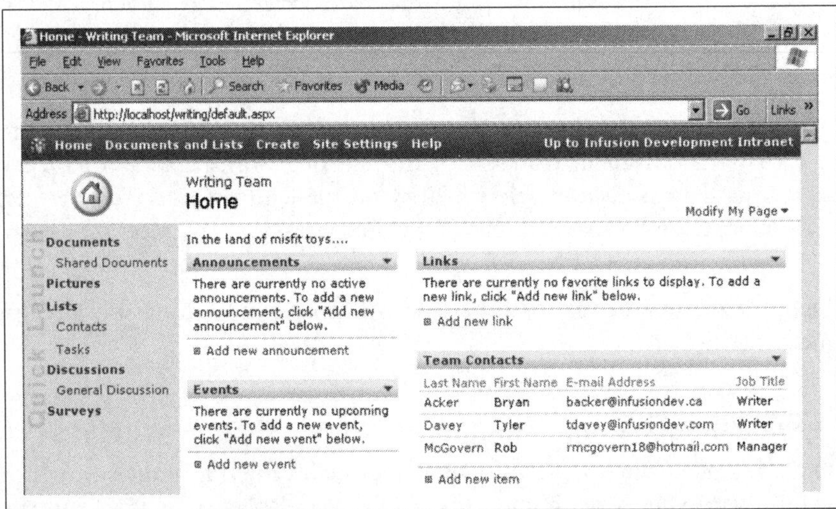

Figure 1-4. Team site home page

Top menu bar

The top menu bar remains the same across all sites and workspaces unless advanced customization tactics are used. The top menu bar provides links to the following areas:

Home
: A link back to the home page of the site.

Documents and Lists
: A link to the Documents and Lists main page. From here, you can manage all documents and lists within the site.

Create
: A link to the Create page. From here, you can create new Web Parts, including:

  - Document libraries
  - Picture libraries
  - Lists
  - Custom lists
  - Discussion boards
  - Surveys
  - Web pages

  Each of these items is described in Chapter 2. You must have appropriate access rights to create any of the above items. Access rights are discussed in Chapter 4.

Site Settings
: A link to the Site Settings main page. From here, you can manage your personal information and the site settings you have permission to modify.

Help
: A link to the Help main page. Help appears in a new window, and allows the user to browse for help while still accessing the site.

Up to <SharePoint Main Site Name>
: A link back to SharePoint's main site.

Quick Launch menu

The Quick Launch menu is found on the navigation bar located on the left-hand side of a SharePoint page and provides most of your navigation needs for accessing libraries and lists. Any library or list can be added and removed from the Quick Launch menu. This provides you with full control over the contents in the menu.

The Quick Launch menu is organized into five categories on the home page:

Documents
: Quick links to all document libraries.

Pictures
: Quick links to all picture libraries.

Lists
: Quick links to all lists.

Discussions
: Quick links to all discussions. Although the Web parts are called discussion boards, the quick launch bar always references these parts as Discussions.

Surveys
: Quick links to all surveys.

Each of these items is discussed in Chapter 2.

When you browse a SharePoint team site, the links on the Quick Launch menu change depending on the page being viewed. For example, when you select the Documents link on the Quick Launch menu, the menu changes to display the Select a View and See Also links.

The biggest change to the Quick Launch menu occurs with meeting workspaces. A meeting workspace does not have a Quick Launch menu. Instead, the workspace has tabs that provide the navigation for the site.

Main content

With the top and the lefthand side of a page devoted to site navigation, the remaining part of the page contains the main content of the site. The main content of a site is always changing, depending on which page you are viewing.

The home page main content area provides sections that a user typically needs to access immediately. For example, in a meeting workspace, the main page contains sections for attendees, agendas, objectives and documents.

With sufficient privileges, you can add and remove these sections in your personal view or for all users. Customization is discussed later in this chapter.

From the home page, you can navigate to pages that display a single item or Web Part. For example, from a "Writers Team" site, you might link to a page displaying a discussion on a particular book project, as shown in Figure 1-5.

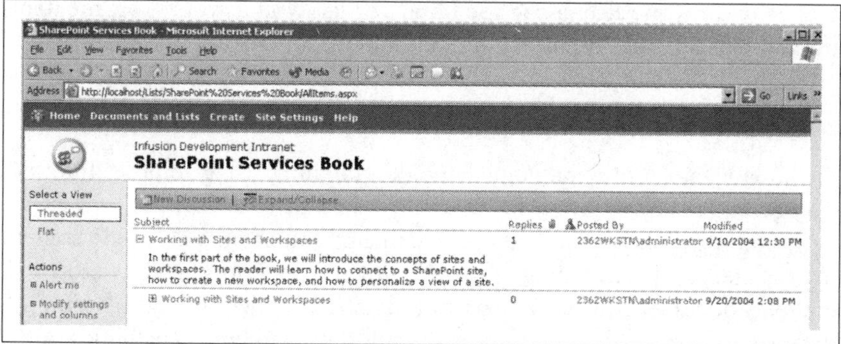

Figure 1-5. A page displaying a discussion board item

Single-item pages display a limited set of choices. For example, on the discussion board page, you can only perform tasks that relate to the discussion, such as viewing an existing thread or creating a new discussion.

Other secondary pages contain Web Parts that have a wider range of choices. Figure 1-6 shows a Documents and Lists page. This page displays the libraries and lists that are available to users. Once you select a specific library or list, you will see a new page that looks more like a single-item page.

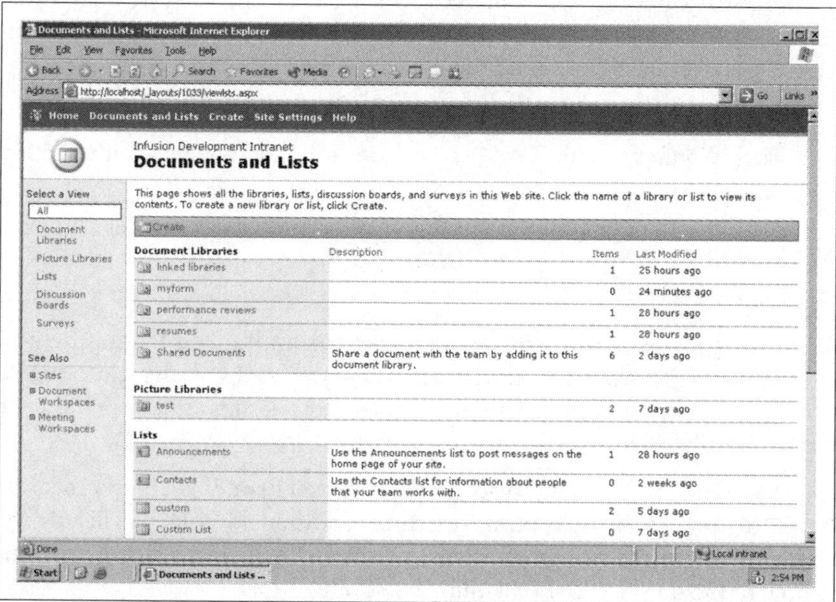

Figure 1-6. Options available on the Documents and Lists page

Not only can you select a specific library or list, you can also sort the items in each section by description, number of items, or last modified date.

Searching a Site

Previous versions of SharePoint handled searching using Internet Information Services (IIS) catalogs. IIS catalogs index documents within a file system, limiting your search to those documents rather than all of the content in the site. To fix this limitation, Windows SharePoint Services stores all content, documents, and settings in a database. Now, instead of using IIS catalogs to search, SharePoint uses the full-text searching capabilities of the database. Searching the database ensures that all content, documents, and settings are searched.

> Search is limited to installations of SharePoint using Microsoft SQL Server 2000 as the database. Microsoft SQL Server Desktop Engine 2000 (WMSDE) does not support searching. For more information on choosing a database, see Chapter 6.

Enabling and disabling searching

In order to search a SharePoint site, you need to enable searching within SharePoint. Only site administrators can enable or disable the search setting. To enable or disable searching:

1. Open the SharePoint Central Administration site.
2. Click Configure Full Text Search from the Component Configuration section.
3. Click the "Enable full-text searching and index component" checkbox.

Searching a site

With searching enabled, a new search text box appears on the top right of all site pages. To execute a search, enter a search string in the text box and click on the arrow button. Figure 1-7 shows the results of a search on the Search Results page.

You can click on any result to access the returned item. If you performed the search within a subsite, you can search for additional results by clicking the "Search for <search string> on <main site title>" link. This will expand your search to include all the sites within SharePoint.

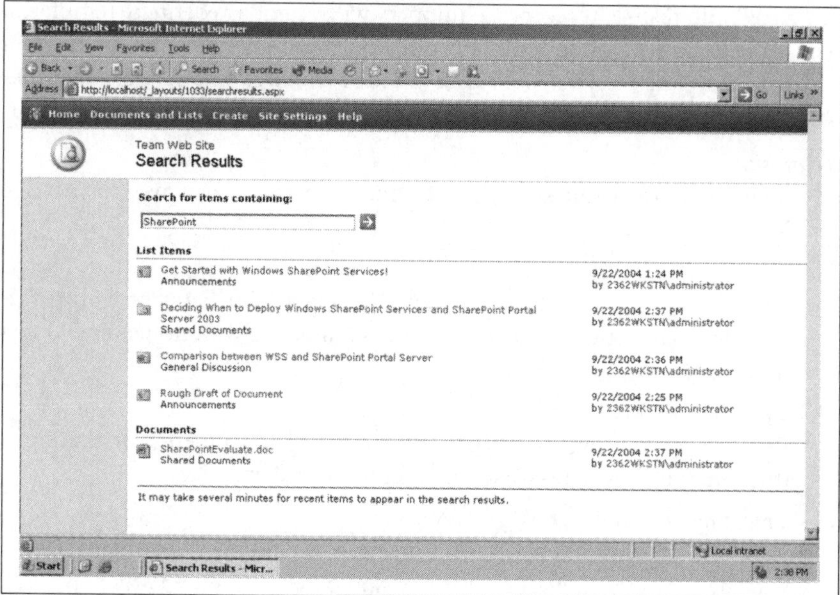

Figure 1-7. The Search Results page

Creating Your Own Sites

Once a team site has been created for your company or group, you can create additional sites and workspaces. SharePoint places no restrictions on the number of sites you create; however, you may be limited by the quality of the hardware on which the site resides. Larger, more powerful computers with more memory can host more sites than smaller, less powerful machines.

When you create your own site, you will usually choose a *site template* that automatically generates a predefined layout. Once the site is in place, you can modify it by adding additional Web Parts, rearranging its layout, or performing other customizations.

Using a Predefined SharePoint Template

A site template provides a default structure and starting point for creating a team site. Some companies use a site template to ensure that a consistent style is maintained throughout all of its SharePoint sites. Even after a template is implemented, you can still make modifications to the site by adding additional Web Parts or by changing the site layout.

A SharePoint team site comes equipped with eight predefined templates. You can use any of these templates for your own site, or you can create a new site template for your own use. Windows SharePoint Services includes the following default site templates:

Team site
: Includes both document libraries and lists teams can use to manage information.

Blank site
: Using a web page editor, you can add SharePoint Services features to your site. This option leaves you with a blank site with no features on its home page.

Document workspace
: Provides everything necessary for managing documents, including a document library, a task list, and a links Web Part.

Basic meeting workspace
: Provides the basic skeleton for a meeting, including a document library and the list items attendees, agenda, and objectives Web Parts.

Blank meeting workspace
: Similar to a blank site, a blank meeting workspace gives you full customization over the meeting site.

Decision meeting workspace
: Provides everything necessary to manage decisions, including everything in a basic meeting workspace with the addition of the decisions list Web Part.

Social meeting workspace
: Provides everything necessary to manage social occasions, including picture library, attendees, discussions, directions, images, and things to bring Web Parts.

Multipage meeting workspace
: Provides a basic meeting skeleton, including agenda, attendees, and objectives, and two blank pages for customization.

Anyone with permission to create a new site can create one with a site template. To implement a site template:

1. Click on the Create link on the top link bar.
2. Select Sites and Workspaces.
3. Enter the following information:
    - The title of the site
    - The description of the site

- The URL of the site
- The user permissions mode

4. Click the Create button.
5. Select a template from the Template list on the righthand side. Figure 1-8 shows the Template Selection page.
6. Click OK.

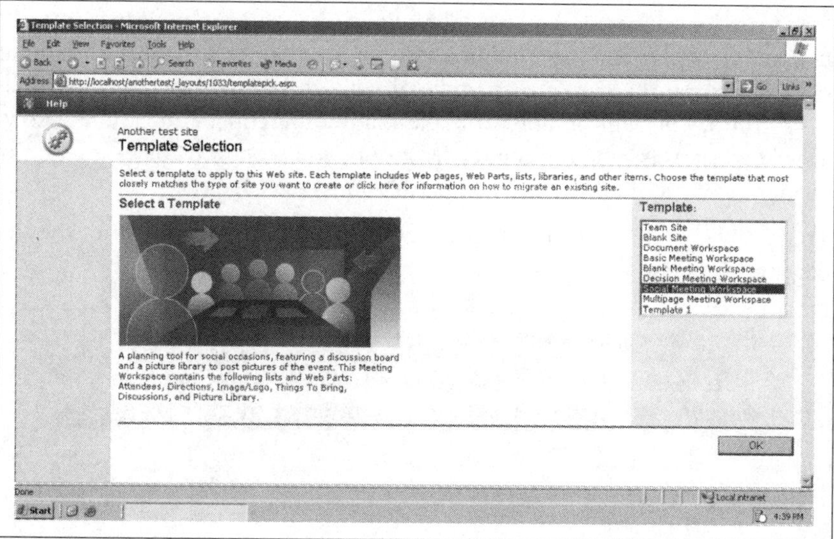

Figure 1-8. Template Selection screen

Using Custom Site Templates

If the eight default templates are not sufficient to meet your needs, you can create a custom site template. The process of creating a custom site template requires that you have administrator-level permissions for the site.

To create a custom site template:

1. Click Site Settings on the top menu bar.
2. Select Go to Site Administration under the Administration section.
3. Click "Save site as template" under the Management and Statistics section.
4. Enter the following information into the form that is displayed:
   - The filename to use for the site template in the File name text box.
   - The title to use for the template in the Template title text box. This will appear in the template gallery selection box.

- A description for the template in the Template description box.
- Optionally, you can include all the content that currently exists in the site. To do this, select the Include content checkbox.

5. Click OK.

Modifying a Site

Once you have created your own SharePoint site, you can modify it through its Site Settings page. The modifications you can make will depend on your permissions on the site. For example, if you are assigned to the web developer group, you will be able to make many different modifications. However, if you are assigned to the reader group, you won't be able to make any changes. For more information on permissions, see Chapter 4.

To modify a site, select the Site Settings link on the top menu bar of the site page, as shown in Figure 1-9.

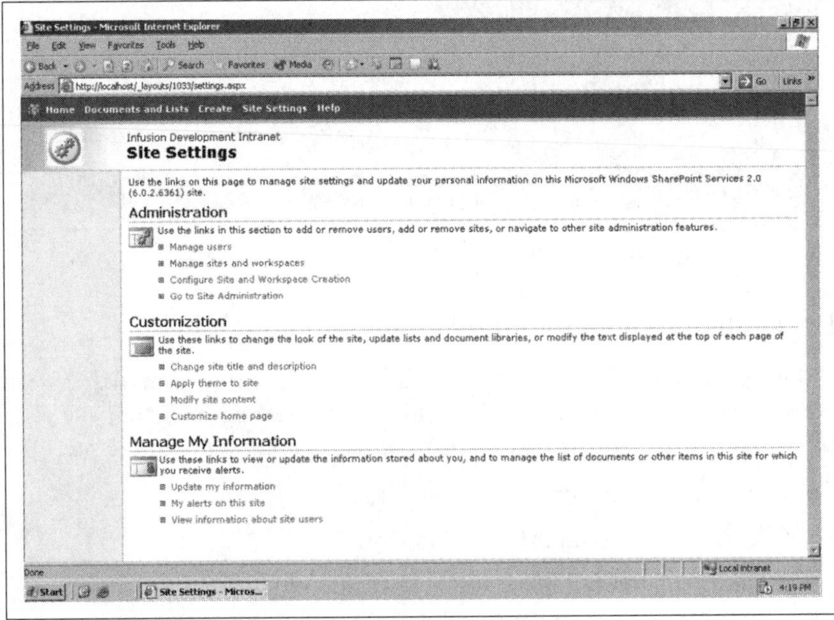

Figure 1-9. A Site Settings page

The following options are available under the Customization section:

Change site title and description

To change the title and description of a site:

1. Select "Change site title and description."
2. Enter the title of the site in the Title text box and the description of the site in the Description text box.
3. Click OK.

Apply theme to site

Themes are special color packages that can drastically change the look and feel of a site. Themes are discussed in more detail in the section "Personalizing a Site." To apply a theme to a site:

1. Select "Apply theme to site."
2. Select a theme from the theme list box.
3. Click the Apply button.

Modify site content

To modify the content of a site:

1. Select "Modify site content."
2. The screen shows all the lists, document libraries, discussion boards, and surveys that are available. From this screen, you can customize any of these Web Parts or create a new content item.
3. Click on an existing content item to modify the item.
4. Click "Create new content" to be brought to the Create Page section.

Customize home page

In design mode, you can modify the Web Parts on the site home page, including their appearance and layout. Any changes made here will be applied for all users.

1. Select "Customize home page," which will take you to the site home page in design mode.
2. In order to change the home page for your personal view, see the section "Changing the Arrangement of Web Parts on a Page" later in this chapter.

Creating Extra Pages

In addition to letting you modify a site you create, SharePoint also allows you to add pages to your team site. By creating additional pages, you can customize the design of pages in your team site. A basic page looks and acts like an HTML page; however, you can design it entirely within the

SharePoint environment. Chapters 2 and 3 discuss how to create more complex pages that require the use of Web Parts.

To create an extra page:

1. Click on the Create link on the top menu bar.
2. Click on Basic Page under the Web Pages section.
3. Enter a name and select a save location for the new web page and click Create.
4. The Rich Text Editor dialog box appears. Use this form to design the page, adding tables, text, links, and other items.
5. Click the Save button.

You might, for instance, create a custom page containing a simple HTML table, such as the Web Part page shown in Figure 1-10.

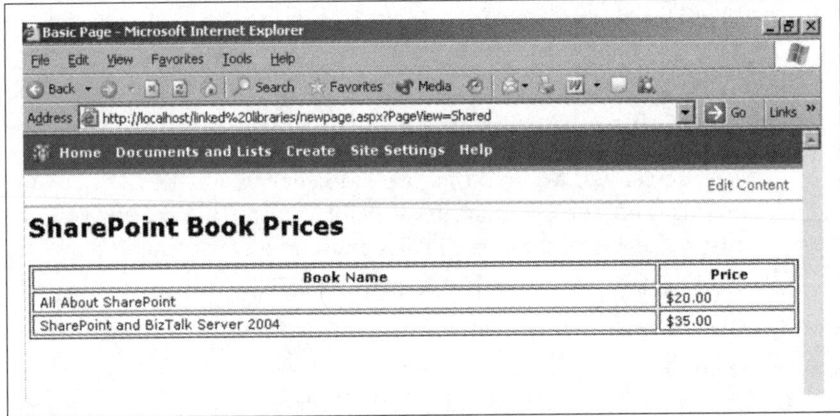

Figure 1-10. A sample extra page

Note that the table shown in Figure 1-10 is coded in pure HTML. You can easily create such content using the Web Parts described in Chapters 2 and 3 of this book.

To view the page you created, navigate to the section you specified as its save location. For instance, if you saved the additional pages in the Linked Libraries section, you could access the page by:

1. Click on Documents and Lists from the top menu bar.
2. Select Linked Libraries under the Document Libraries section.
3. Click on the page you created.

Figure 1-11 shows an additional page in the Linked Libraries section of the team site.

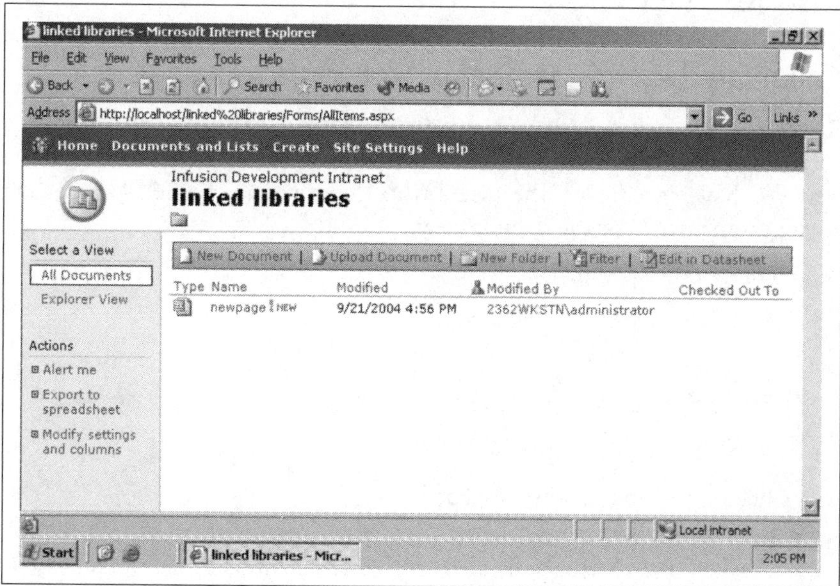

Figure 1-11. Extra page location

Note that some users may have rights to modify the page you created. If another user modifies the page, you would see the user's name in the Modified By column. Similarly, a user may check the page for editing. For more information on the version control built into a library, see the section "Library Web Parts" in Chapter 2.

Personalizing a Site

For a user, the layout and design of a site is just as important as the content. A user will want the ability to make the site his own by choosing a layout and styles that suit his personality. SharePoint supports personalization that allows users to:

- Modify a site
- Move Web Part locations
- Apply themes
- Add alerts

Some or all of these personalization features may be limited by the user's specific permission level within a specific site. For more information on permissions, see Chapter 4.

Changing the Arrangement of Web Parts on a Page

Through your personal view you can change the layout of Web Parts on a team site page. Whenever you view the page, you will see it displayed the way you have specified. Other users who view the page will either see their own personal view, or the default view.

SharePoint allows you to:

- Delete Web Parts
- Add new Web Parts
- Change the location of Web Parts on the screen

To modify the layout of a page:

1. Click on the link Modify My Page.

> If you belong to the web designer or administrator site group for the site, the link may say Modify Shared Page. Click on the link and select Personal View before selecting Modify My Page.

2. Select the option "Design this page" in the menu that appears. SharePoint changes the page to design mode.
3. Drag and drop Web Parts from one location to another to create your personal view. Remove Web Parts from the screen by clicking the X button.

Figure 1-12 shows a team site home page displayed in design mode. Notice that while in design mode, the main content is surrounded by two frames: Left and Right. You can move any Web Part from the Right side to the Left side by simply dragging and dropping.

Modifying the Settings of a Web Part

In design mode you can also modify the settings of a Web Part. If you have the proper site permissions, you can change the appearance, layout, and custom features of any Web Part. To modify a Web Part:

1. Click on the down arrow inside the Web Part title bar.
2. A list of options appears. Select Modify My Web Part.
3. The screen changes to resemble Figure 1-13.

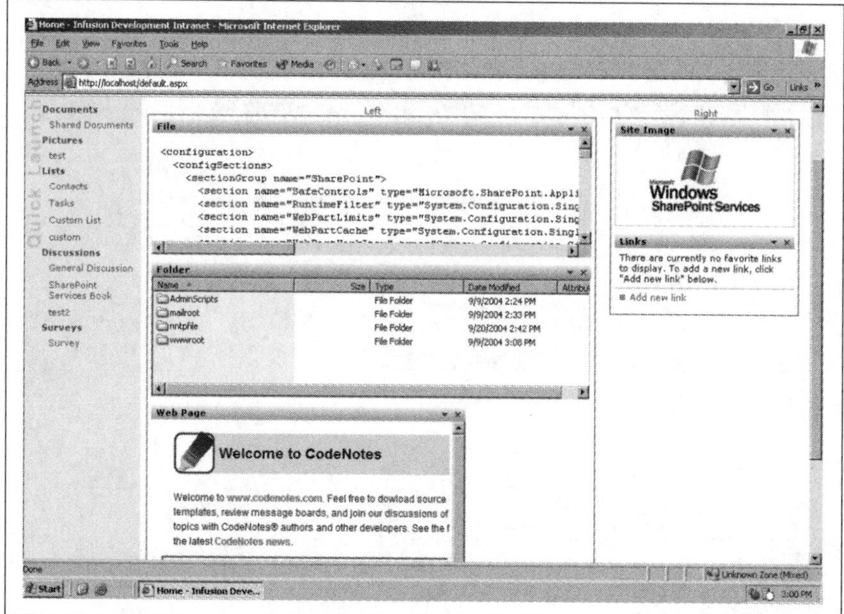

Figure 1-12. Page layout modification mode

4. On the righthand side of the screen you can specify the modifications to the Web Part. In this section, you can change the appearance, layout, and custom options for the Web Part.
5. Click OK.

All the modifications you make are only visible when you view the page. None of your personal modifications will change the view other users see.

Applying Themes

Themes allow you to apply a uniform site style across an entire site. Only users assigned to the web designer or administrator site group can create a theme and apply it to a site. When a theme is applied to the site, every user will see the same theme.

Themes are custom style sheets that, when applied to a site, change the colors, fonts, and overall appearance of the site. SharePoint ships with twenty default themes that you can choose from. You can also create a custom theme through Microsoft FrontPage and add it to the list of available themes. Creating a theme is beyond the scope of this book and requires advanced development knowledge.

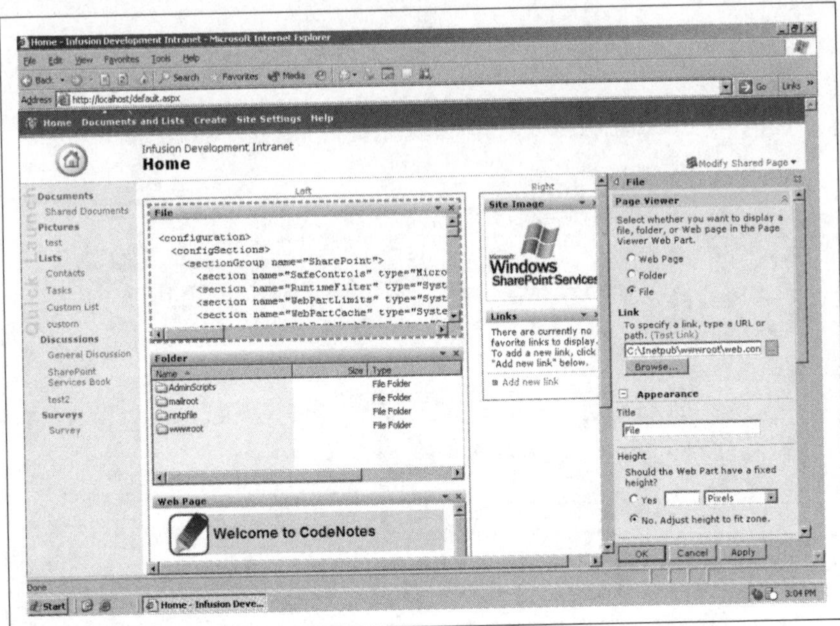

Figure 1-13. Web Part modification

To apply a theme to a SharePoint team site, perform the following actions:

1. Click the Site Settings link on the top link bar.
2. Select "Apply theme to web site" under the Customization section. Figure 1-14 shows the Apply Theme to web site page.
3. Select one of the themes on the righthand side. The team site will preview on the lefthand side with the new theme.
4. Click the Apply button to assign the theme to the site.

To remove a theme, follow the first two steps mentioned above. At Step 3, select No Theme (Default) and click the Apply button.

Setting Alerts

As a user, you can set an alert to notify you by email if a particular piece of content changes. You can create an alert to track the following items:

- Document libraries
- Documents
- Picture libraries
- Images

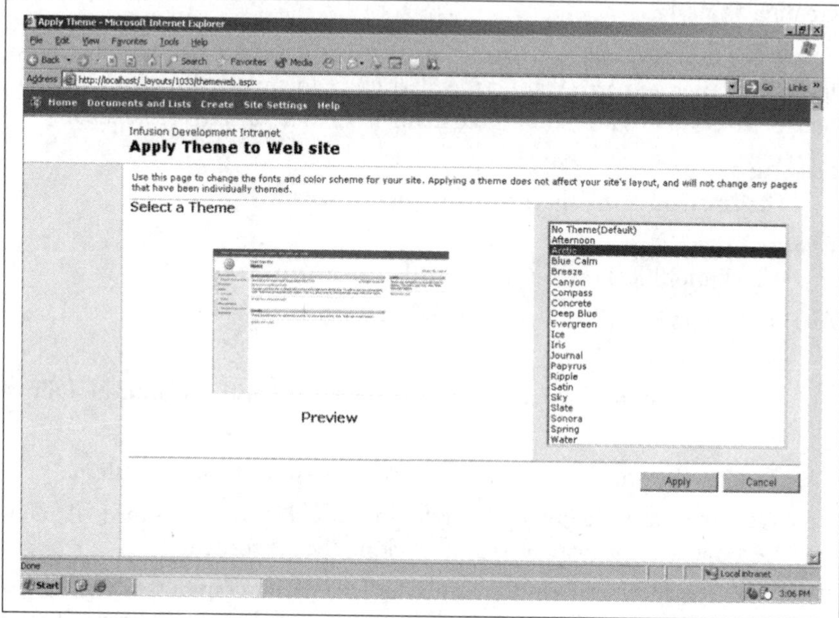

Figure 1-14. Applying a theme

- Lists
- List items
- Discussion boards
- Discussion messages
- Surveys

For example, a user may decide to sign up for an alert on a discussion board. If any other user posts a response to a discussion item, or creates a new item, the first user receives an email notification. This feature is particularly useful for discussion board moderators.

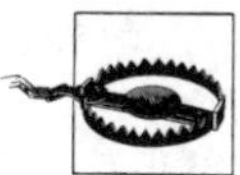

The only drawback to alerts relates to security. If you delete a user or remove a user's access rights from content in SharePoint, the user will continue to receive alerts that he created on that content. To fix this situation, the administrator must remove all alerts that the user originally created on the content.

Creating an alert

The procedure you follow to create an alert is similar for all content, regardless of whether you are creating the alert for a document, list, discussion, or image. You will need to fill in three main areas of a form to create an alert:

Send Alerts To
: The email address where the alert will be sent

Change Type
: Which modification to the item will create an alert

Alert Frequency
: How often to be notified

To add an alert to an item such as a document library, perform the following steps:

1. Click on the document library to which you want to add the alert.
2. Select the Alert Me link on the lefthand side. Figure 1-15 shows the New Alert page that is displayed after clicking the Alert Me link.
3. Your email address is pulled from the SharePoint configuration information. You should always verify that the email address is correct. If your email address is incorrect, click on the "Change my e-mail address" link to change your email address.
4. Select the type of changes that you want to be alerted to under the Change Type section. The alert type options include:

   All changes
   : Whenever a change is made, you are alerted.

   Added items
   : Whenever a new item is added, you are alerted.

   Changed items
   : Whenever an item is modified, you are alerted.

   Deleted items
   : Whenever an item is deleted, you are alerted.

   Web discussion updates
   : Whenever a web discussion based on this library is updated, you are alerted.

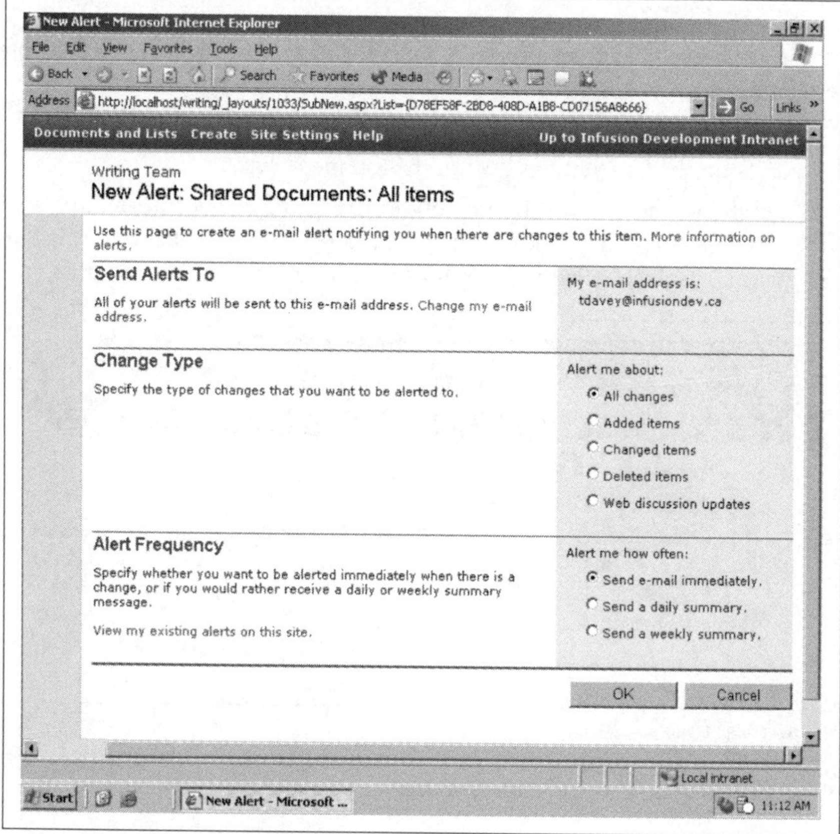

Figure 1-15. Adding an alert to a document library

5. Select how often you want to receive alerts under the Alert Frequency section. The alert frequency options include:

   Send e-mail immediately
   : At defined intervals (five minutes is the default), SharePoint sends out immediate alerts. You will receive an email at the default interval time whenever any change is made.

   Send a daily summary
   : You will receive a daily email summarizing all changes. If no changes occurred during a day, you won't get an email.

   Send a weekly summary
   : You will receive an email once a week summarizing all changes. Once again, if no changes occurred during the week, you won't get an email.

Viewing your alerts

Once you have created an alert for yourself, you may need to delete the alert or change the settings of the alert. SharePoint lists all of your alerts for a site on the My Alerts page. To view your alerts for a site:

1. Click on the Site Settings link on the top menu bar.
2. Select "My alerts on this site" under the Manage My Information section. After selecting "My alerts on this site," the My Alerts on this Site page is displayed. Figure 1-16 shows the My Alerts on this Site page.

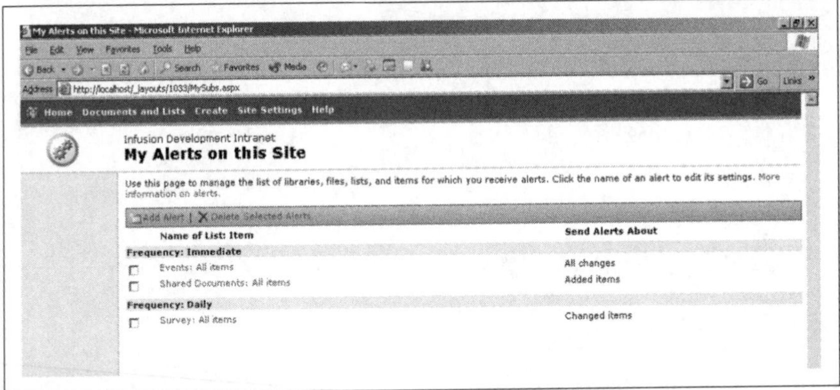

Figure 1-16. Viewing all alerts

On this page, you can add, edit, and delete your alerts.

Deleting an alert

To delete an alert or a group of alerts from your My Alerts page:

1. Select the checkbox beside each alert that needs to be deleted.
2. Click the Delete Selected Alerts button.
3. Select OK when the message box appears to confirm the deletion.

Adding an alert

To add an alert to your My Alerts page, click the Add Alert button.

Clicking the Add Alert button brings up the New Alert page displayed in Figure 1-17:

1. Select which list or document library for which you wish to create an alert. Alternatively, you can view the items in the list or document library to add an alert for an individual item.
2. After selecting the list or document library, click Next.
3. Follow Steps 3–5 in the section "Creating an alert" to fill in the form, then select OK.

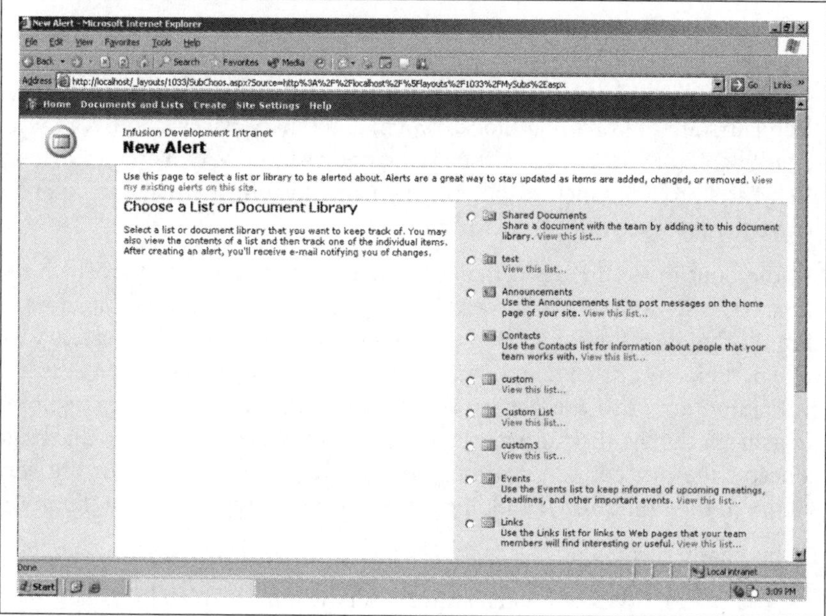

Figure 1-17. Creating a new alert from View Alerts screen

To edit the settings of an alert:

1. Click on the name of the alert you wish to edit.
2. You can modify the same options that you set during the creation processed outlined in the section "Creating an alert."
3. Click OK to save the changes or Delete to delete the alert.

CHAPTER 2

Basic Web Parts

Web Parts are the building blocks of a SharePoint Services site. Every Windows SharePoint Services site consists of one or more Web Parts. Individual Web Parts provide functionality ranging from document storage to complex data entry forms to discussion forums.

All the built-in Web Parts actually derive from the concept of a list. In the most basic sense, a list is a Web Part that displays a sequence of information. In the SharePoint world, the list concept covers everything from a list of hyperlinks to a discussion board. In every case, the end user views the list, adds information to the list, modifies information on the list, or removes items from the list. Because all the built-in Web Parts derive from this basic concept, the procedure for adding an issue to an issue Web Part are very similar to the procedure for adding a new document to a document library.

In this chapter, you will:

- Learn about the common features of all the built-in Web Parts
- Work with advanced, list-based Web Parts including issues lists, discussion boards, surveys, and custom lists
- Learn how to use library-based lists to control documents and pictures
- Explore advanced features of the built-in Web Parts, including access controls, custom views, and list templates

What Is a Web Part?

A Web Part is a modular and reusable component that can be placed into any SharePoint Services web page. A Web Part is generally composed of a

Web Part description file (*.dwp*) and some external code that provides the functionality (a .NET assembly or *.dll* file). For most purposes, however, all you need to know is that a Web Part is a building block for a team site.

The Web Part Description

The Web Part description file is an XML file containing all the property names and settings for the Web Part. The description file also contains a reference to the Web Part assembly. In general, you will never have to look at or understand a DWP file unless you are developing your own custom Web Parts.

The Web Part Code

Each Web Part is a special type of ASP.NET application. The Web Part code is compiled into a .NET assembly and stored in the Global Assembly Cache or the *bin* directory. Once again, unless you are developing your own custom Web Parts, you will never need to look at the code files for a Web Part.

Basic List Functions

A SharePoint Services list is a collection of information that can be shared by team members. All SharePoint sites include a set of built-in lists that can be filled with any required team information. You can also create custom lists based on existing list formats or those that follow your own formats.

In this section, you will:

- Learn about the types of SharePoint lists available to users
- Learn how to work with the features common to all SharePoint lists

Types of Web Parts

SharePoint Services offers six simple list-based Web Parts, plus custom lists, discussion boards, and surveys. All of these Web Parts share similar functionality for adding, sorting, and removing items.

Basic lists

The basic list Web Parts provide standard list functions. The primary differences between these Web Parts are the different columns that are displayed in the list, and how you add data to the list. The six basic list Web Parts are:

Links
: A links list is a list of hyperlinks to web pages that are useful to site users. A site administrator might create a links list for standard resources needed by the team.

Announcements
: An announcements list is designed as a place to post any team-related information (for example, notifying users of a new group member). Figure 2-1 shows an announcements list. All the basic lists share similar structure and layout.

Contacts
: A contacts list contains the name, address, phone number, and email address of any people whom a user may need to contact during a project. One interesting feature of the contacts list is that it can be integrated with Microsoft Outlook. In other words, you can populate a contacts list by synchronizing it with your Outlook mailbox.

Events
: The events list is a list of any dates that are important to the team (for example, product launches or meetings).

Tasks
: The tasks list is a to-do list for site users. Each task is presented as its own list entry.

Issues
: The issues list is designed to help manage outstanding project problems. Issues can be assigned to a specific user and can be prioritized by severity. The issues list is explained in the section "Advanced Web Parts" later in this chapter.

Custom lists

If none of the basic lists meets your needs, you can create custom lists in one of three ways:

Custom lists
: When you create a custom list, you define the columns and select the data types. SharePoint will automatically generate a form for filling the list with data.

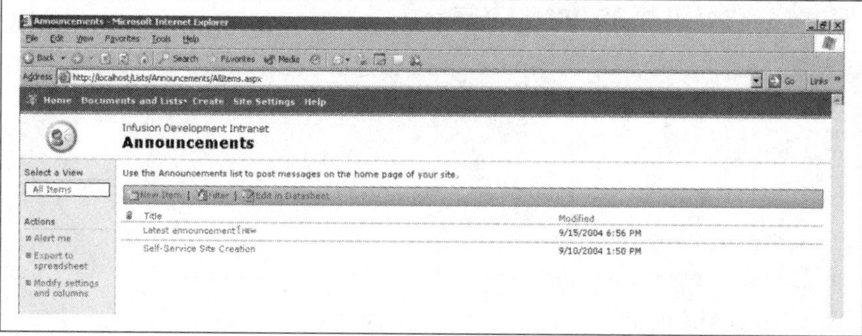

Figure 2-1. Announcements list

Custom list in a datasheet view
: If you want a list that looks like a spreadsheet, you can create a custom list in a datasheet view. This type of custom list provides a spreadsheet-like environment for convenient data entry, editing, and formatting. In order to create a datasheet view, you need a Windows SharePoint Services-compatible list datasheet control such as Microsoft Excel, and ActiveX control support.

Import a spreadsheet
: If you have a SharePoint Services compatible program (for example, Excel 2003 or Internet Explorer 5.0 or greater) you can create lists from spreadsheets. SharePoint Services imports your data and displays the information as a list.

The tasks necessary for building a custom list are explained in the section "Advanced Web Parts."

Other Web Parts

Although the survey and discussion board Web Parts share many features with the basic lists, these Web Parts are treated separately because they offer more complex features:

Surveys
: A survey Web Part is a specialized list that combines features of the simple lists with a system for tracking answers from site users.

Discussion boards
: A discussion board is essentially an improved issues list that allows interactive discussion between team members.

Both surveys and discussion boards are explained in the section "Advanced Web Parts."

Working with Standard Lists

All the built-in lists share similar core functionality. Regardless of the list type, you will use the same basic procedures to:

- Create the list
- Add information to the list
- Edit the contents of the list
- Delete content from the list
- Change the name or description of a list
- Attach files to a list

Creating a standard list

To create any of the built-in list types:

1. Click Create in the top link bar.
2. Select the type of list you want to create (for example, "Links").
3. Type a name for the list in the Name text field.
4. Type a description of the list in the Description text field. This step is optional.
5. If you want the list to appear in the Quick Launch bar, select the Yes radio button in the Navigation section.
6. Click Create.

Adding information to a list

The steps to add information to a built-in list are very similar for each of the built-in lists—i.e., the steps to add announcements are very similar to the steps to add links or events to a list. This example outlines the steps required to add an announcement to an announcement list:

1. Click on Documents and Lists in the top link bar. You will see a new page similar to Figure 2-2.
2. Click Announcements in the lists section.
3. Click New Item. Figure 2-3 shows the Announcements: New Item page that is used to create a new announcement.
4. Type a title in the Title text field.
5. Type the body of the announcement in the Body field.
6. If you want the announcement to be displayed for only a certain period of time, click on the Calendar control and select an end date.
7. Click Save and Close.

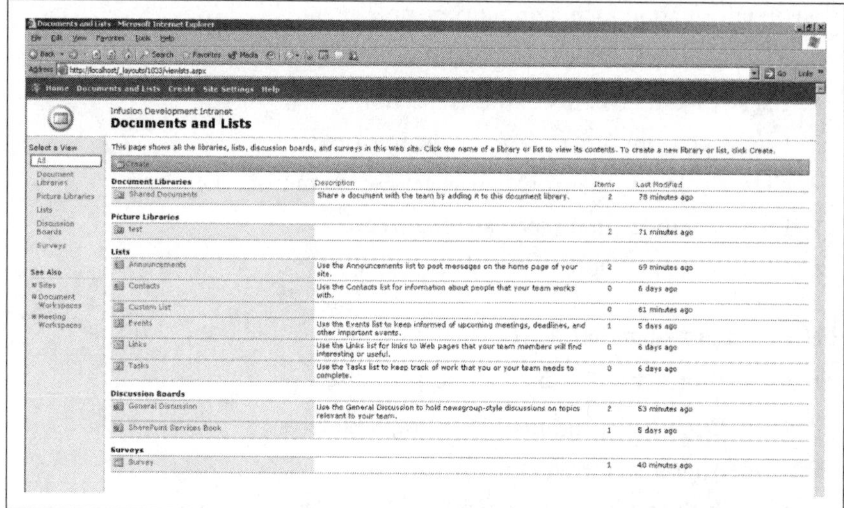

Figure 2-2. Documents and Lists page

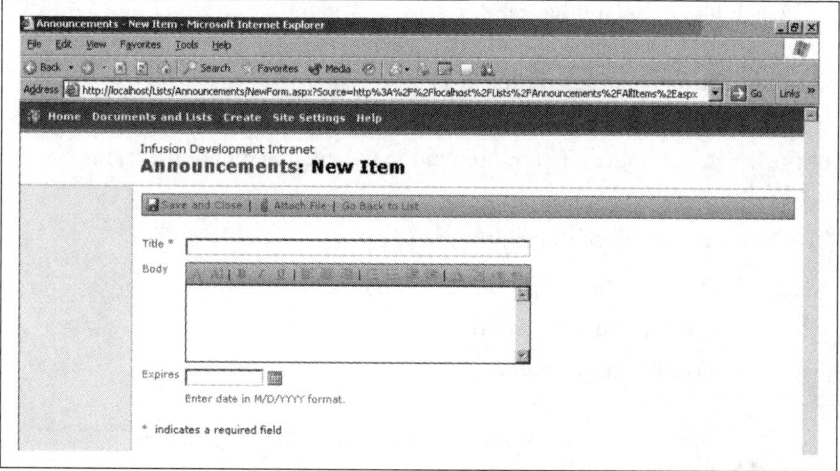

Figure 2-3. Add a list item page

Remember that adding information to any list will follow the same basic steps. However, the data entry form will be slightly different depending on the list type.

Editing information in a list

Editing information in a list follows a set of steps similar to adding the information. Keep in mind that all lists will use similar steps; however, the actual fields may be different.

To edit information in an announcement list:

1. Click Documents and Lists in the top link bar.
2. Click Announcements in the list section.
3. Point to the announcement you want to edit.
4. Click on the down arrow and select Edit Item from the menu.
5. Edit the information you want changed.
6. Click Save and Close.

Deleting information from a list

To delete information in an announcement list:

1. Click Documents and Lists in the top link bar.
2. Click Announcements in the list section.
3. Point to the announcement you want to delete.
4. Click on the down arrow and select Delete Item from the menu.
5. Click OK to delete the item.

Changing the name or description of a list

As people start adding information to a list, you may find that the purpose of the list has changed. Therefore, you may need to update the name of your list Web Part or the description.

To change the name or description of a list:

1. Click Documents and Lists in the top link bar.
2. Select the list you want to edit.
3. Click "Modify settings and columns."

If the page displays a survey, click "Change survey and questions."

4. Under General Settings, click "Change general settings."
5. Edit the information for Name and Description.
6. Click OK.

Attaching files to a list item

In certain cases, you may want to attach a file to specific list items. For example, if you create a task list for new employees, you can attach a health benefits form to the step requiring each employee to sign up for insurance.

You can attach files to existing items or attach a file when you create a list item.

To attach a file to an existing item:

1. Click Documents and Lists in the top link bar.
2. Click on the list that you want to attach your file.
3. Select the existing list item.
4. Click the down arrow and select Edit Item from the menu.
5. Click Attach File.
6. Browse to the file you want to attach to the item and click Open.
7. Click the OK button.
8. Click Save and Close.

To attach a file to a list item when you create the item:

1. Click Documents and Lists in the top link bar.
2. Click on the list that you want to attach your file.
3. Click New Item.
4. Type the title and any additional required information.
5. Click Attach File.
6. Browse to the file you want to attach and click Open.
7. Click OK.
8. Click Save and Close.

Advanced Web Parts

Once you understand the basic functions of a list-based Web Part, you can start to work with any of the built-in Web Parts. However, some of the more advanced Web Parts expose additional functions that are above and beyond the basic behavior of a list. In this section, you will learn about:

- Issues list
- Discussion boards
- Surveys
- Custom lists

Each of these Web Parts builds on the basic list parts by offering advanced features designed for the specific functions of the Web Part. For example, issues lists provide a special set of columns for tracking project-related issues. Similarly, surveys are designed to collect specific information from each user and present the results.

Finally, if none of the basic lists meets your needs, you can create your own lists by defining the columns, data types, and look and feel of the list.

Issues Lists

Issues lists are designed to help you manage any outstanding problems on a project. You can assign issues to specific team members, prioritize issues, and track the progress of any issue on the project.

Each issues list displays a table with default columns specific to tracking issues in a project. Table 2-1 details the default columns of an issues list.

Table 2-1. Issues list columns

Column name	Functionality
Add related issue	Displays the Issue ID for any issues related to the specific issue.
Assigned To	Indicates which user is assigned to the issue.
Attachments	If a file is attached to the issue, the filename is displayed in this column.
Category	Organizes issues into three categories.
Comment	A brief description of the issue.
Created	The timestamp that indicates when an issue was created.
Created By	Indicates which user created the issue.
Current	Displays two checkboxes (Yes or No) to inform if an issue is still current.
Due Date	The projected date by when the issue must be resolved.
Edit	Displays the edit icon to users. If a user clicks on the edit icon, she is taken to the Edit Issue page.
Issue ID	A unique identifier that is automatically generated by SharePoint Services. The Issue ID cannot be changed.
Modified	The timestamp that indicates when the issue was last modified.
Modified By	Displays the user ID of the last person to edit the issue.
Priority	Allows a user to set the issue as a high, normal, or low priority. By setting priority, users can focus on the most important issues.
Status	Indicates if an issue is active, resolved, or closed. Users can filter lists to display only active issues so they can focus on out standing tasks.
Title	Displays the title for an issue.

The issues list offers the same core functionality as other simple lists. You can add or delete issues lists in the same fashion as any other built-in lists. You can add, edit, delete, or attach a file to an item in any issues list. You can also alert a user when any assigned issue changes.

Issues list specific features

An issues list allows you to perform several tasks that are not available in other built-in lists. These tasks include:

Adding or removing a related issue
: This feature lets you assign or remove issues to an existing user. Any added issue will be displayed in the list of issues on the user's home page. Conversely, any removed issues are deleted from the user's issue list.

Assigning an issue to a user
: Assigning an issue to a user links the user to the issue, puts the issue on the home page for that user, and sets up an alert to notify the user that the issue has been assigned.

Viewing issue history
: A user can easily view the history of any project issue, including changes in status, comments, any users that modified the issue, and the current status of the issue.

Viewing related issues
: A user has the option to view any existing issues that are related to the current issue. For example, if a user is assigned to an issue that relates to a specific customer, the list can be configured to allow the user to view any other issues that relate to that customer.

Resolving, closing, or reactivating an existing issue
: Users can change the status of any issue in the issues list. If a user has proper permissions, he can close or reactivate an issue. An Issues list can be sorted to display all issues, or to display only specific types of issues.

Turning on/off email notification
: When the email notification is turned on, a user will receive an email anytime a new issue is assigned, or when the status of an existing issue changes.

Viewing issues list reports
: SharePoint Services issue lists can be configured to create easy-to-read issue reports. An issues list report can list all of a project's issues, the status of each issue, and what user is assigned to the issue.

Discussion Boards

Discussion boards are used as a forum to discuss any topics that interest users on your team site. Most sites use discussion boards to pose questions to team members or plan activities. For example, if you have an issue with a block of code, you can post a question to all your team members on the discussion board.

Discussion boards include the buttons and functionality for users to start new discussions, reply to existing discussions, and sort and filter any existing discussions. Users can also switch the design and view of the discussion board. Figure 2-4 shows a standard discussion board Web Part.

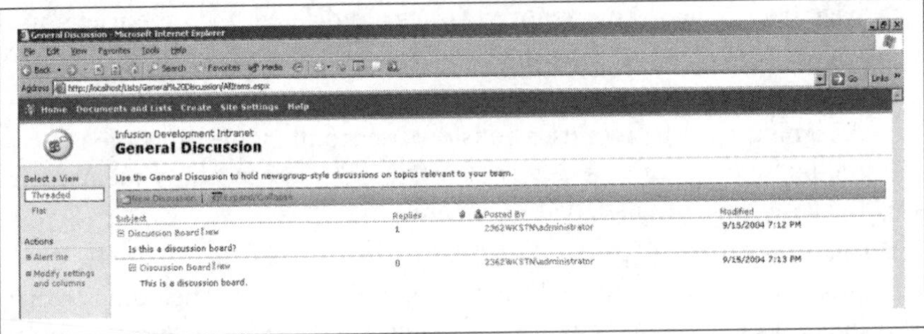

Figure 2-4. Discussion board

You can set up the discussion board to alert users when the discussion board is changed and to display the discussions in threaded or flat views. A threaded view sorts all comments by conversation. All comments from a single discussion are listed in the order they were created. A flat view displays all comments in the order they were created, regardless of the associated discussion. Although you can set a default view, each user can choose to switch to any other established view.

Creating a discussion board

Creating a discussion board is slightly more involved than creating any of the simple list Web Parts. To create a discussion board:

1. Click Create in the top link bar.
2. Click Discussion Board on the Create page.
3. Type a name in the Name text field.
4. Type a description in the Description text field. This step is optional.
5. If you want the discussion board to appear in the Quick Launch bar, select the Yes radio button in the Navigation section.
6. Click Create.

Start a discussion

Once the board is created, any authorized user can start a new discussion. To start a discussion:

1. Click Documents and Lists on the top link bar.
2. Click the name of the desired discussion board.
3. Click New Discussion.
4. Type the discussion title in the Subject text field.
5. Type your comment in the Text text field.
6. Click Save and Close.

Reply to an existing comment

If you want to reply to a comment in an existing discussion:

1. Click Documents and Lists on the top link bar.
2. Click the name of the desired discussion board.
3. Navigate to the comment to which you want to post a reply.
4. In the Subject column, click the down arrow, and select Reply from the menu list. This will launch the General Discussion: New Item page (Figure 2-5).
5. Type your reply in the Text field.
6. Click Save and Close.

Figure 2-5 displays the New Item page for discussion board Web Parts.

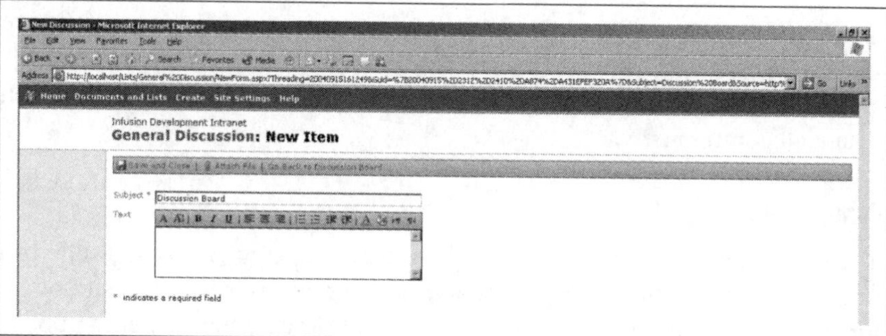

Figure 2-5. Replying to an existing discussion

Edit comments

A site administrator can configure a discussion board such that a user can edit any previously posted comments. The option to edit all comments or just the user's own comments must be configured by the site owner.

To edit an existing comment:

1. Click Documents and Lists on the top link bar.
2. Click the name of the desired discussion board.
3. Navigate to the comment you want to edit.
4. In the Subject column, click the down arrow, and select Edit Item from the menu list.
5. Edit the existing text.
6. Click Save and Close.

Depending on your permission level, you may not be allowed to edit any comments, you may be allowed to edit only your own comments, or you may be allowed to edit any comments. If you are a site owner, you can control this setting using the steps in the section "Controlling Access."

Delete a discussion comment

To delete a discussion item:

1. Click Documents and Lists on the top link bar.
2. Click the name of the desired discussion board
3. Navigate to the comment you want to delete.
4. In the Subject column, click the down arrow and select Delete Item from the menu list.
5. Click OK.

Once again, permission to delete comments is controlled by the owner of the site. You might not be allowed to delete any comments, you might be allowed to delete only your own comments, or you might be allowed to delete all comments.

Content approval

The site owner can also configure a discussion board to ensure that inappropriate content is not posted. By requiring content approval, the site owner forces all new comments to enter an approval process before being publicly displayed.

Site administrators and users with the manage lists permission can:

- Accept or reject content
- Include comments as to why the specific content was rejected
- Add content without having it approved

Note that rejecting content does not mean users cannot view their pending content. Users can always view any of their own pending items. To prevent users from viewing pending items, a site administrator or a user with "manage list" permissions must manually delete the content.

Surveys

The SharePoint Services survey Web Part provides you with an easy tool to poll site users. You can create a survey by adding questions and requiring team members to respond. Figure 2-6 shows a standard survey Web Part. The survey Web Part allows you to easily compile survey results and view the results in a graphical summary view.

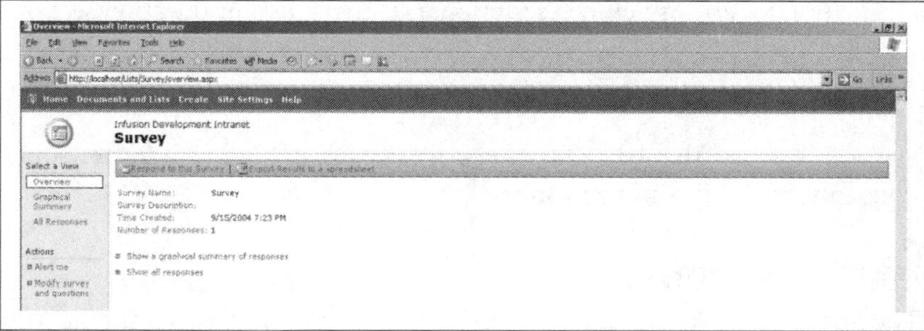

Figure 2-6. Survey Web Part

Create a survey

Survey creation is usually a site administrator task. Therefore, you may not have permission to create new surveys. If you are the site administrator, or you have the "manage lists" permission, you can create new surveys on a site.

To create a survey:

1. Click Create in the top bar link.
2. Click Survey.
3. Type a name for your survey in the Name text box.
4. Type a description that explains the purpose of the survey in the Description text field. This step is optional.
5. If you want the survey to appear in the Quick Launch bar, select the Yes radio button in the Navigation section.
6. If you want the respondent's name to be visible to all users, select the Yes radio button in the Show user names in the survey results section.

7. If you want users to be able to reply to the survey more than once, select the Yes radio button in the Allow multiple responses section.
8. Click Next.

Adding a question to a survey

Once again, only site administrators and users with the correct permissions can add questions to a survey. To add a question to your survey:

1. Navigate to the Add Questions page.
2. Type your question in the Question text box.
3. The Survey Web Part includes functionality for you to determine the format for the answers to questions. You can specify the type of information for an answer in the Optional settings for your question section.
4. To add more questions, click Next Question and repeat steps 2 and 3.
5. Click Finish to save your survey.

Figure 2-7 shows the Add Question page, which is used to add new questions to surveys on your team site.

Responding to a survey

The SharePoint Services survey Web Part displays a survey as a simple form that users complete. Every user can respond to a survey.

To respond to a survey:

1. Click Documents and Lists in the top link bar.
2. In the Surveys section, click on the survey you want to complete.
3. Click "Respond to this survey."
4. Complete the survey.
5. Click Save and Close.

To see the results of a survey

SharePoint Services compiles all survey results and displays the results in a graphical summary. To view the graphical summary:

1. Click Documents and Lists in the top link bar.
2. In the Surveys section, click on the survey whose results you want to view.
3. Click Graphical Summary under the Select a View section.

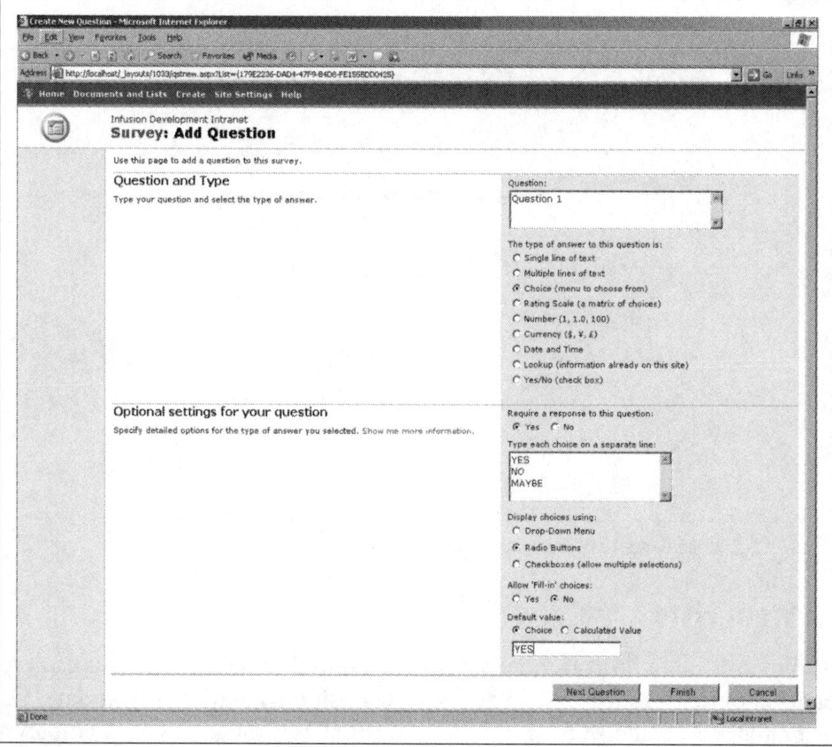

Figure 2-7. Adding a question to a survey

To see how specific users responded to a survey

Depending on how the site administrator configured the survey, you may be able to see either generic results or user-specific results to the survey (see Figure 2-8). If the site administrator indicated that the respondent's name should be visible, a username will be included with each set of survey results.

To see how other users responded:

1. Click Documents and Lists in the top link bar.
2. In the Surveys section, click on the survey whose results you want to view.
3. Click All Responses under the Select a View section.
4. Click View Response #n.

Figure 2-8 shows a typical survey results screen.

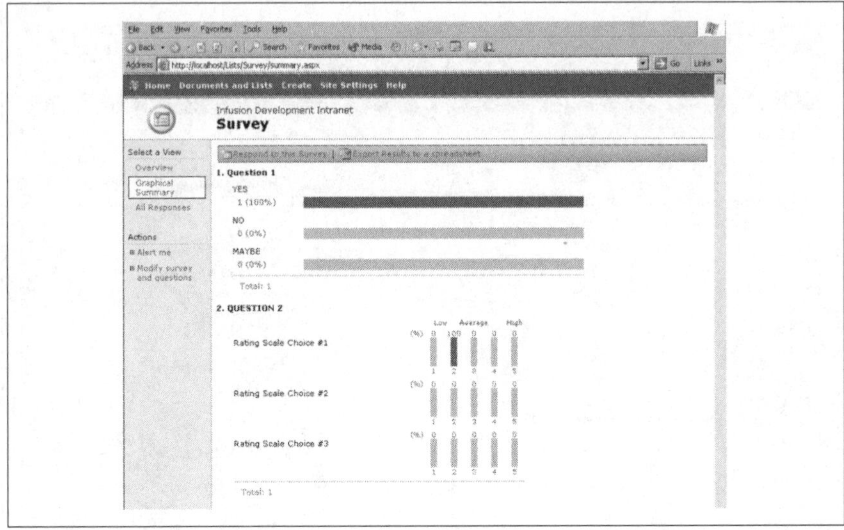

Figure 2-8. Survey results screen

Custom Lists

If none of the built-in lists matches your desired functionality, you can create custom lists that will display your own columns and your own data. For example, you could build a custom list that shows the hours each employee worked per week. Figure 2-9 displays a custom list that shows how many hours overtime each employee worked, and how much overtime pay each employee is owed. The list uses a formula column to determine both the number of overtime hours worked and the amount of overtime pay each employee is owed. The amount owed field also uses a lookup column to search the site for each employee's hourly wage.

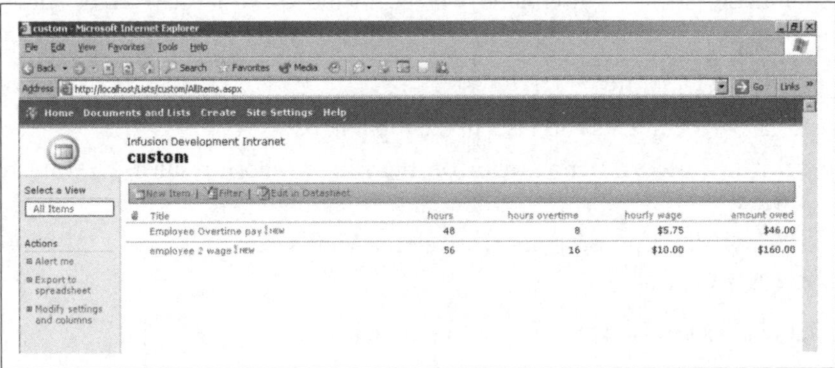

Figure 2-9. Custom list

As you might expect, creating a custom list is much more involved than creating an ordinary list.

Create a custom list

To create a custom list:

1. Click Create in the top link bar.
2. Click "Custom list."
3. Type a name in the Name text field.
4. Type a description in the Description field.
5. If you want your custom list to appear in the Quick Launcher bar, select the Yes radio button in the Navigation section.
6. Click Create.

Adding columns to a custom list

Completing the preceding steps creates a blank custom list. To add columns to your custom list:

1. Navigate to the page that displays your custom list.
2. Click "Modify settings and columns."
3. Click "Add a new column" in the Columns section. This will bring up the Custom List: Add Column page (Figure 2-10).
4. In the Name and Type section, type a name for the column and select the type of information you want to display.
5. Specify the appropriate settings in the Optional Settings for Column section.
6. Click OK.
7. Repeat the preceding steps for each column.

Each column in a list can display single or multiple lines of text, numbers, currency, the date, yes/no fields, hyperlinks, or pictures. SharePoint Services also has several custom information types:

Choice
: A choice type forces users to select from pre-existing values, similar to a drop-down list. You can add a choice field to a custom list by selecting the choice radio button from the Name and Type list. In the Optional Settings for Column section you can add the choices you want displayed in the list. You can also choose how the choices are displayed in the list (for example, drop-down menu, radio buttons, or checkboxes), and whether you want users to be able to fill in any other choices.

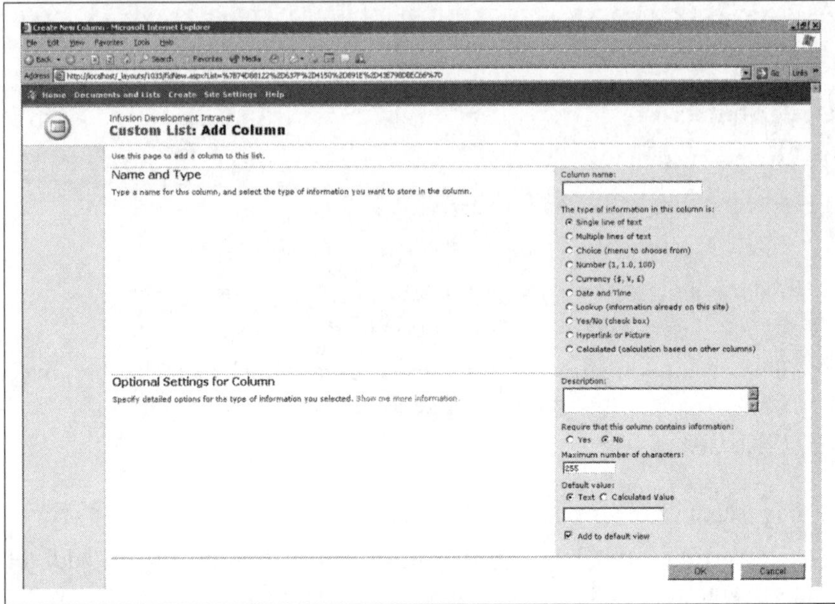

Figure 2-10. Adding a column to a custom list page

Lookup
: A lookup information type retrieves a value from an existing list or library and displays the value. You can add a lookup field to a custom list by selecting the lookup radio button from the Name and Type list. The Optional Settings for Column section lists all existing lists and libraries for your site. To add a lookup field, you must select a list or library and the associated field you want to display.

Calculated
: A calculated information type displays values that are derived from a formula. Formulas can use dates, numbers, or existing list and column values. When you create a custom list, you can add a formula column by selecting the calculated radio button from the Name and Type list. In the optional settings section, you can create a formula by entering information in the formula text area. A formula can be a combination of existing columns, operators, and constants.

Create a custom list in datasheet view

In order to create or use a list in datasheet view, your computer must have certain software installed. Specifically, you will need Microsoft Office Professional Edition 2003. More specifically, you need the Microsoft Office List Datasheet Component, which is an ActiveX control bundled into the Office

2003 installation. If you have this component, and you are using Internet Explorer 5.01 (SP2) or higher, and have ActiveX controls enabled for your SharePoint site, you can create a list in datasheet view.

To create the list:

1. Click Create in the top link bar.
2. Click Create Custom List in Datasheet View.
3. Type a name in the Name text field.
4. Type a description in the Description field.
5. If you want your custom list to appear in the Quick Launch bar, select the Yes radio button in the Navigation section.
6. Click Create.

Once the list has been created, you can define the columns and add data just as if you were using Microsoft Excel.

Create a custom list by importing a spreadsheet

You can import an existing Microsoft Excel spreadsheet as a custom list. To create the list:

1. Click Create in the top link bar.
2. Click Import Spreadsheet.
3. Type a name in the Name text field.
4. Type a description in the Description field.
5. Click the Browse button and navigate to your spreadsheet. The spreadsheet must be in Microsoft Excel format.
6. Click Import. This will open up a new wizard that will help you determine what you wish to import.

Library Web Parts

Quite often you will want to add a Web Part to share documents between the members of the site. The library Web Parts are enhanced lists specifically designed for storing, controlling, and maintaining various types of documents. A SharePoint Services library displays all the files stored in the library. The library also lists the properties for each file and provides a hyperlink to open the file. Using the library Web Parts, a site administrator can also implement version control on the items in the library. That is, an end user will have to specifically "check out" a document before editing it. When the editing is complete, the user can "check in" the document, incrementing the version number. Any user can see all the versions of the document and compare changes between versions.

In this section, you will learn about:

- The views associated with library Web Parts
- The specific features of a document library
- The specific features of a picture library
- Version control

The Home Page

Every library Web Part presents a home page view that includes the links necessary to work with the library and one of several views of the content in the library. From the library home page, you can:

- Add files and folders to the library
- Sort and filter files contained in the library
- Switch the library view
- Change the design of the library
- Create alerts so users are notified of any changes in the library or specific files within a library

When you add or remove files from the library, the associated hyperlinks are automatically updated.

Document Libraries

Document libraries are collections of files that allow a team to share files. A document library is basically a file repository for any documents that you want to share with your team. You can upload documents to the library, as well as edit existing documents in a controlled versioning environment. Document libraries allow you to create and save documents in standard templates. One possible use of a document library is to store all customer invoices. Figure 2-11 shows a standard document library.

The all documents view

The default view displays all documents in the library in a simple table. You can either work with each document in this view or click the Edit in Datasheet link if you need to make mass changes to the library. The datasheet view provides you with an Excel-like interface with improved features for copying, pasting, mass selecting, and deleting library components.

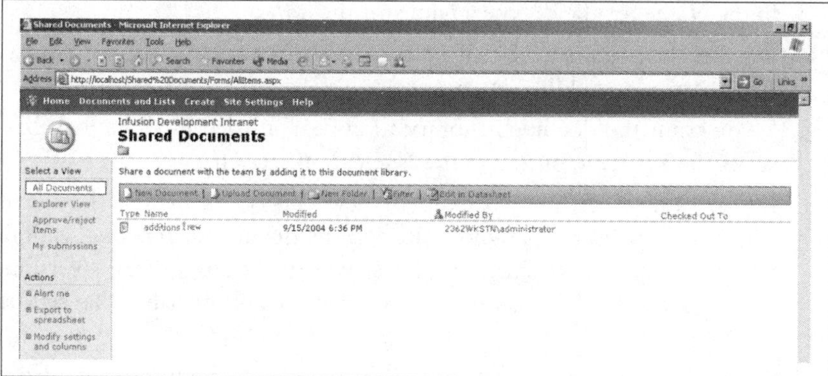

Figure 2-11. A document library (all documents view)

The explorer view

All libraries include an explorer view that mirrors the functionality of the Microsoft Windows Explorer. The explorer view lets you delete, rename, or copy and paste files and folders. Figure 2-12 shows a standard document library in explorer view.

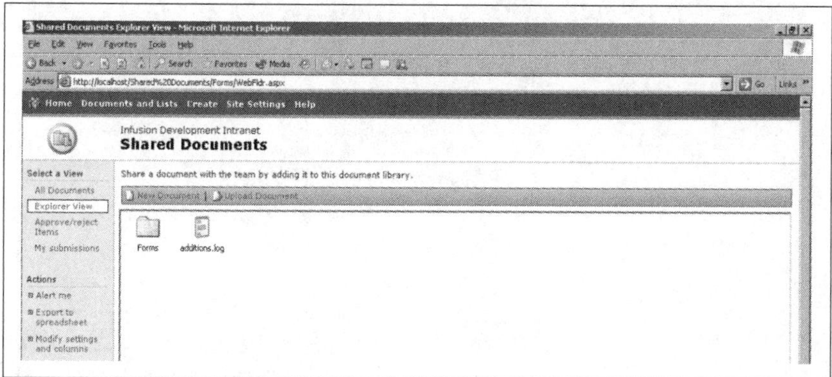

Figure 2-12. Library in explorer view

Within the explorer view you can drag and drop files from a regular Windows Explorer instance into your SharePoint site. However, your site administrator may have set up permissions that restrict the use of this view.

Creating a document library

To create a document library:

1. Click Create on the top link bar.
2. Click "Document library" on the Create Page page.

3. In the Name text field, type a name for the library.
4. On the Description text field, type a brief description for the library. The description field is not required.
5. If you want the document library to appear in the Quick Launch bar, select the Yes radio button in the Navigation section.
6. If you want to create a backup or new version each time the file is edited, selected the Yes radio button in the document Versions section. Site users can access either the latest version or any previous version. See the section "Version Control" for more details on what this setting means.
7. Select a default document template from the document template drop-down menu. The default document template determines the format of any new file created in the document library.
8. Click Create.

Figure 2-13 shows the New Document Library page that is used to create new document libraries on your team site.

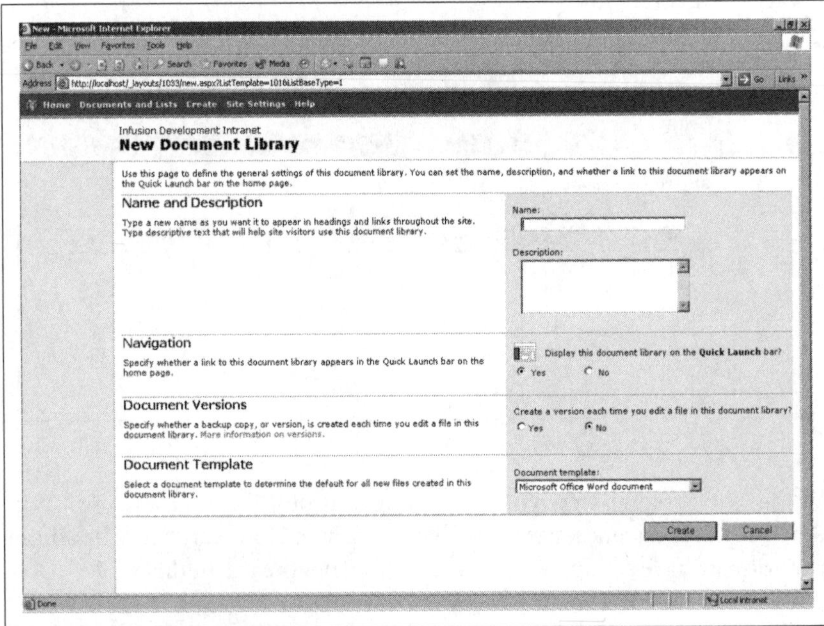

Figure 2-13. Create a document library

Your document library will be added to your site. You can now add files to the library using either the upload button or the explorer view.

Document templates

To enforce consistency for your document library, you can specify a template to be used anytime a new document is created. You can create templates for any SharePoint Services–compatible program. To use a template, the template must be stored in the site template gallery.

For example, you can attach a Microsoft Word template to a document library. Whenever a user creates a new Microsoft Word document within the library, he will automatically be forced to use the attached template. If you have a Microsoft PowerPoint template for slides, you could attach it to the document library so that all Microsoft PowerPoint presentations will automatically have the same look and feel.

Adding documents to a document library

To add a document to a document library:

1. Click Documents and Lists in the top bar link.
2. Click on the document library in which you want to add the document.
3. Click "Upload document."
4. In the Upload document page, click the Browse button and navigate to the file you want to upload.
5. If a document with the same name already exists in the document library and you want to overwrite the file each time a new version is saved, click the "Overwrite existing file(s)?" checkbox.

As an alternative, you can use the explorer view and drag and drop, or copy and paste your files from a Windows Explorer instance into the document library (or vice versa).

File formats in a document library

When you create a document library, you can save your files in binary format or in a web-based format. Both options have advantages and disadvantages. If you use a program-specific format (for example, *.doc*, .or *.xls*) you retain the runtime features of the program, but users must have the appropriate program installed to view the files.

If you use a web-based format, team members aren't required to have the appropriate program installed, but some runtime functionality might be lost.

Picture Libraries

Picture libraries provide the functionality for you to share and organize images in a corporate server environment. Picture libraries mirror the functionality of document libraries. Both types of libraries allow users to edit, copy, and delete files from the repository.

Picture libraries display photos in three different styles. A picture can be displayed as a thumbnail (a small version of the picture), filmstrip (displays both a smaller version of the picture and a larger, more detailed version of the picture) or as picture details (the actual picture is not displayed, just the associated picture information).

For example, several picture libraries could be used to store all the photos taken by photographers at a newspaper. By creating a picture library for each photographer, any reporter working on a story related to the pictures could access the picture library without having to search for the correct files. Figure 2-14 shows a standard picture library.

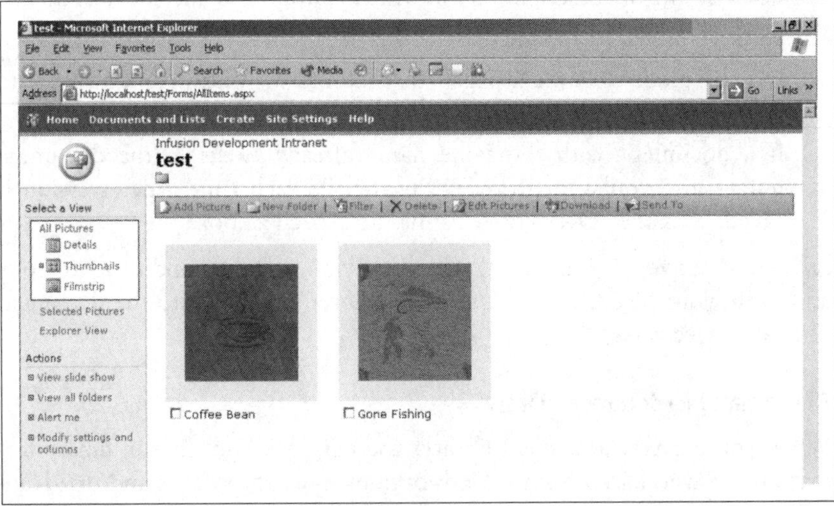

Figure 2-14. Standard picture library

Although pictures can be stored in other types of SharePoint lists, using a picture library lets users:

- Look at pictures in different views (All pictures, Selected pictures, and Explorer)
- Share pictures using slide shows
- Send pictures directly to Microsoft Office 2003 programs

- Download pictures directly to your computer
- Edit pictures with a Windows SharePoint Services–compatible image editor

Creating a picture library

To create a picture library:

1. Click Create on the top link bar.
2. Click "Picture library."
3. Type the name of the picture library in the Name text field.
4. Type a brief description of the picture library in the Description text field. This step is optional.
5. If you want the picture library to be visible in the Quick Launch bar, select the Yes radio button in the Navigation section.
6. If you want to create a backup of a picture every time it is checked into the picture library, select the Yes radio button in the picture Versions section. See the section "Version Control" for more details on what this setting means.
7. Click Create.

Figure 2-15 shows the New Picture Library page that is used to create new picture libraries on your team site.

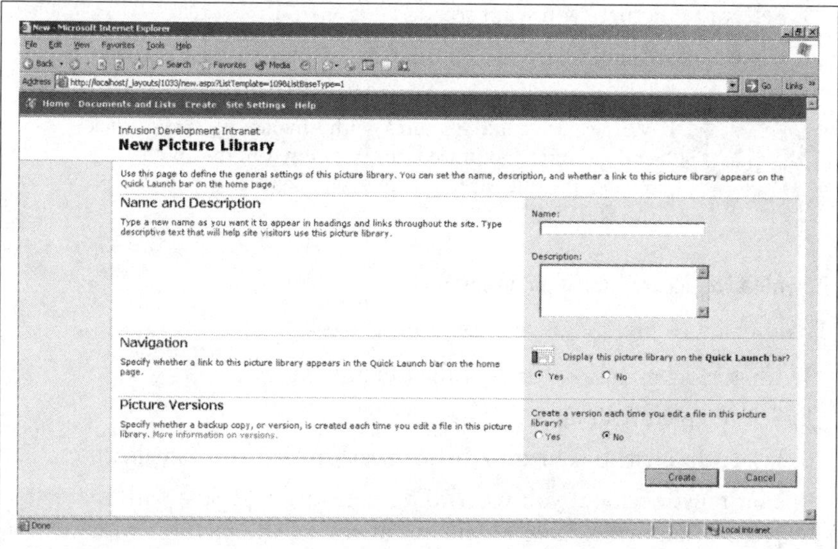

Figure 2-15. Create a picture library page

Adding pictures to a picture library

To add a picture to a picture library:

1. Click Documents and Lists in the top link bar.
2. Click the name of the specific picture library.

At this point, you can upload a single picture or multiple pictures.

Adding a single picture

To add a single picture to a picture library:

1. Click "Add picture" in the picture library.
2. Click Browse and navigate to the picture you want to add to the library.
3. Click Open.
4. If a file with the same name already exists in the library, you must decide if you want to overwrite the existing file.
5. Click Save and Close.

Adding multiple pictures

To add multiple pictures to a picture library:

1. Click "Add picture" in the picture library.
2. Click Add Multiple Files.
3. Select the pictures you want to add.
4. Click Upload and Close to add the pictures in their original size.

If you want to add pictures with smaller file sizes, click "Send pictures optimized for viewing on the Web." By reducing the file size, pictures will load faster in a web browser.

Download a picture from a picture library

To download a picture to your computer:

1. Click Documents and Lists in the top link bar.
2. Select a picture library.
3. Select the checkbox next to the pictures you want to download.
4. You must decide if you want to download the photos with the default picture settings or if you want to download the pictures with customized settings (for example, setting the width and height properties).

5. Click Download.
6. If you want to download the pictures to a specific location (as opposed to the default location), click Browse and navigate to the location where you want to store the files.

Version Control

Implementing version control allows you to save multiple versions of a document on your server. When you enable document versioning for a document library, a backup copy of your file is saved each time the file is saved to the library. This feature is useful in case you have to revert to an older copy of the file or you want to keep a history of any changes that are made to the document. If you have documents that need to be edited by several users, saving the original version of the file is very helpful to keep track of each user's modifications.

By turning on versioning, you can:

- View previous versions of the file
- Restore a file to a previous version
- Delete all previous versions of a file
- Restore deleted files
- Force document check-in

Versioning can be applied to all files except HTML. In order to version web documents, you must use the MHTML format.

Implementing version control

If you are the site administrator and did not enable version control when you created your library, you can turn it on later by adjusting the settings for your library.

To enable version control:

1. Navigate to your library.
2. Click on the Modify Settings and Columns link.
3. In the General Settings section, click on the Change General Settings link.
4. In the Document Versions section, select the Yes radio button.
5. Click OK to apply the changes.

Viewing a previous version of a file

A user can view previous versions of any document in the document library. Figure 2-16 shows the Versions saved page that contains all versioning information for a specific document. To view a previous version of a file:

1. Point to the file in your library.
2. Click the triangle that appears.
3. Click Version History.
4. In the Modified column, click your desired version.

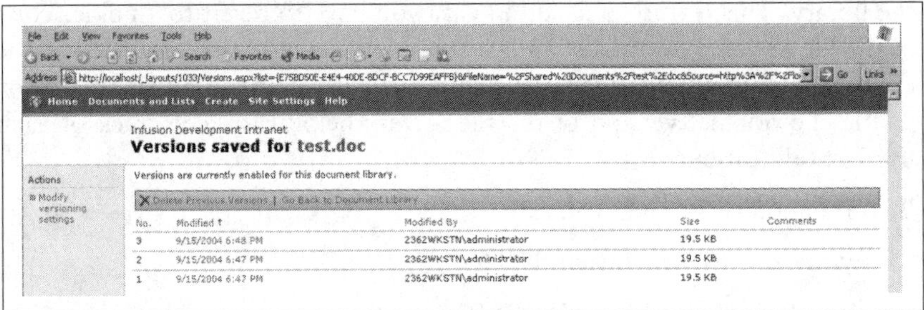

Figure 2-16. Version history for the test.doc document

Restore a file to a previous version

In certain cases, you may want to revert to a previous version of a file. For example, if a user makes unacceptable edits or overwrites important changes, you may need to return to the previous version of the file. To restore a previous version:

1. Point to the file in your document library.
2. Click on the triangle that appears.
3. Click Version History.
4. In the Modified column, point to the version you wish to restore.
5. Click the triangle that appears.
6. Click Restore in the menu that appears.
7. Click OK when asked if you want to replace the file.

Delete previous versions of a file

If you have permission, you can delete one version or all of the previous versions of a file. Previous versions take up space on the hosting server, so although you may want to save previous versions, documents that undergo numerous changes over an extended life cycle can take up large amounts of space. To delete a previous version of a file:

1. Point to the file in your document library.
2. Click on the triangle that appears.
3. Click Version History.
4. In the Modified column, point to the version you want to delete.
5. Click the triangle that appears.
6. Click Delete in the menu that appears.
7. Click OK to confirm that you want to delete the file.

If you delete the file directly, you will also delete all saved versions. The above procedure lets you selectively delete old versions of a file without deleting all of the file history.

Advanced Web Part Features

With all of the Web Parts described in this chapter, a site administrator can configure advanced features, including creating list templates, creating list views, and adjusting the security for accessing a Web Part.

List Templates

When you create a list, you must select a list template that renders the content in a predetermined format. SharePoint Services includes several list templates. Any template can be customized and saved as a new template. Administrators can import new templates to the site and make the new templates available to all users.

By definition, a list template contains all the design information for a list. A template does not contain any security information or general list information. A list template also contains server information (URLs and user account names), so it is crucial that only trusted users are given access to the site list template gallery.

Creating a list template

To create a list template, you must have "manage list" permissions. To save a list as a template:

1. Navigate to the list you want to save as a template.
2. Click "Modify settings and columns" on the Actions page.

3. Click "Save list as template" under the General Settings section of the Customize:<List_Name> page.
4. Type the filename in the File Name text field.
5. Type the title of the template in the Template Title text box.
6. Type a description for the template in the Template Description text field.
7. Select the "Include content" checkbox if you want to include the existing content.
8. Click OK.

Add a template to the site template gallery

In order to add a template to the site template gallery, you must have "add item" permission for the site template gallery. To add a template to the gallery:

1. Click Site Settings on the top-level web site.
2. Click Site Administration in the Administration section.
3. Click "Manage site template gallery" in the Site Collection Galleries section.
4. Click "Upload template gallery" on the Site Template Gallery page.
5. Click Browse and navigate to the template you want to add to the gallery.
6. Click "Save and Close."

Delete a template from the site gallery

To delete a template from the site template gallery, you must have "Add Item" permission for the site template gallery. To delete a template gallery:

1. Click Site Settings on the top-level web site.
2. Click Site Administration in the Administration section.
3. Click "Manage site template gallery" in the Site Collection Galleries section.
4. Click the Edit icon next to the template name.
5. Click Delete.

Managing Views

Views make it quick and easy to see list information in a variety of ways. You can use views in lists, libraries, surveys, and discussion boards. You may notice that certain parts have additional built-in views. For example, a discussion board has a flat view and a threaded view. Similarly, a document library has the all documents view and the explorer view.

You may want to create your own custom views to control the appearance of a Web Part. For example, you may want a view on a contacts list that sorts the contacts by company rather than first name.

Once a view is created, a hyperlink is added to the Quick Launch bar that allows you to view information in a specific view. You can create the following types of views:

Standard view
: The standard view displays the default columns of the list in a simple table format.

Datasheet view
: This view creates an editable spreadsheet format that is good for bulk editing.

Calendar view
: This view displays data in a calendar format.

Figure 2-17 shows an announcements list in a datasheet view.

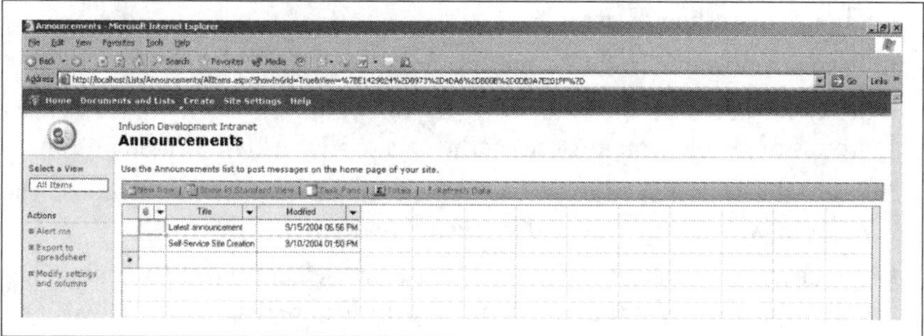

Figure 2-17. A list in datasheet view

Creating a calendar list view

To create a calendar list view:

1. Open the List of Invoices list.
2. Click "Modify settings and columns."
3. In the Views section, click "Create a view."
4. Choose Calendar View.
5. Type a view name in the Name text field.
6. Select an audience for your view. If you want your view to be seen by groups of people, you must select the Create a Public View radio button.
7. Select a column to base the calendar view (for example, modified or created).

8. Select a calendar setting to determine if your calendar list view will appear in month view, week view, or day view.
9. If you want to filter your calendar list view, select up to two columns and conditions (for example, setting Created by ID to be greater than 10) to filter your list.
10. Click OK.

After completing the preceding steps, you can view the List of Invoices list in a calendar view.

Creating a datasheet view

The datasheet view provides you with an easy way to edit information. To create a datasheet list view:

1. Open the List of Invoices list.
2. Click "Modify settings and columns."
3. In the Views section, click "Create a view."
4. Choose Datasheet View.
5. Type a view name in the Name text field.
6. Select an audience for your view. If you want your view to be seen by groups of people, you must select the Create a Public View radio button.
7. Select the columns you want to appear in the list view, and choose the order in which they will be displayed.
8. If you want to sort your datasheet list view, select up to two columns to determine the order that the items in your list are displayed.
9. If you want to filter your datasheet list view, select up to two columns and conditions (for example, setting User ID to be greater than 10) to filter your list.
10. If required, select an items limit, and select whether you want to display the total number of attachments of items in the list.
11. Click OK.

After completing the preceding steps, you can view the List of Invoices list in a datasheet view.

Controlling Access

It is important for a site administrator to control who has access to the information in a list. By controlling access to lists, you can ensure that secure material cannot be viewed by users without the proper permissions. Similarly, you can prevent unauthorized users from adding new documents, deleting existing documents, or modifying documents.

SharePoint Services gives you the ability to control permissions on lists and libraries. (Security is discussed in Chapter 4.) Setting permission on lists and libraries ensures only authenticated users can access secure information. For example, your company may only want members of the human resources group to have access to salary information. You can grant users the following access:

- View items
- View items; edit, delete items
- View items; edit, delete items; change list settings
- View items; edit, delete items; change list settings; change security

You can grant or revoke permissions by user, groups of users, or by site group. Any user with "manage lists" or "Full Control" rights can change the permissions of a list or library.

You can set advanced permissions for specific users or groups. These advanced permissions are:

- Manage lists
- Manage list permissions
- Cancel check-out
- Manage personal views
- Add list items, edit list items, and delete list items
- View list items

Any user with "manage lists" permissions can edit the existing permissions for the specific list or library. Users with this permission can view permissions for a list, change the permissions for a specific site group, assign or remove permissions to a specific user or group, reset permissions to the default settings, and enable anonymous access for the list.

The steps on how to modify permissions for lists and libraries are the same. Therefore, the following procedures show only the steps to change permissions for an example list named "List of Invoices."

View permissions for a Web Part

To view the permissions on the List of Invoices list:

1. Navigate to the List of Invoices list.
2. Click "Modify setting and columns" in the Action pane.
3. Click "Change permissions for this list" in the General Settings section of the Customize list of Invoices page.
4. The Change Permission: List of Invoices page displays the users and groups that can access the list and their assigned permissions.

Change permissions for a site group

A site group is a group of similar users who share a common set of permissions. (Site groups are discussed in Chapter 4.) To change the permissions of a list for a specific site group:

1. Navigate to the List of Invoices list.
2. Click "Modify setting and columns" in the Action pane.
3. Click "Change permissions for this list" in the General Settings section of the Customize list of Invoices page.
4. Select the site group you want to change.
5. Click Edit Permissions of Selected Users.
6. Select the level of permissions you want to allow the group and click OK.

Selectively assign permissions to a specific user or user group

You can selectively assign permissions to a specific SharePoint user, or to a Windows group. Unlike site groups, Windows users and groups are controlled by your system administrator.

To assign user- or group-specific permissions:

1. Navigate to the List of Invoices list.
2. Click "Modify setting and columns" in the Action pane.
3. Click "Change permissions for this list" in the General Settings section of the Customize list of Invoices page.
4. Click Add Users on the list toolbar.
5. In the Step 1: Choose Users section, type the email address or domain name and account name for the group or user you want to assign permissions in the Users area.
6. In the Step 2: Choose Permissions section, select the level of permissions you want to assign and click Next.

7. In the Step 3: Confirm Users section, verify that the email address, user name, and display name are correct.
8. If you want to send an email to a user when you change permissions, select "Send the following email" to let these users know they've been added checkbox in the Step 4: Send Email section, and then add the body text you want sent in the email.
9. Click Finish.

Remove permissions from a user, group, or site group

To remove permissions from a user, group, or site group:

1. Navigate to the List of Invoices list.
2. Click "Modify settings and columns" in the Action pane.
3. Click "Change permissions for this list" in the General Settings section of the Customize list of Invoices page.
4. Select the site group you want to change.
5. Click Remove Selected Users.
6. Click OK.

Restore default permissions

You can restore the default permissions to a list. To return to the default settings:

1. Navigate to the List of Invoices list.
2. Click "Modify settings and columns" in the Action pane.
3. Click "Change permissions for this list" in the General Settings section of the Customize list of Invoices page.
4. Click "Inherit permissions from the parent web site."
5. Click OK.

Grant anonymous access

If your web site is configured to grant access to anonymous users (through IIS), you can grant anonymous users access to a list or library:

1. Verify that your web site grants anonymous access.
2. Navigate to the "List of Invoices" list.
3. Click "Modify settings and columns" in the Action pane.
4. Click "Change permissions for this list" in the General Settings section of the Customize list of Invoices page.

5. Click “Change anonymous access” in the Action pane.
6. Select the checkbox that corresponds to the level of permissions that you want to grant to anonymous users.

If IIS is not configured to allow anonymous users, the checkboxes will not be visible.

7. Click OK.

CHAPTER 3

Extending Site Pages

SharePoint Services includes features that allow you to extend the functionality of a basic team site. SharePoint Services implements Web Parts to link to external web sites, system folders, or files, as well as allow users to configure how the content is displayed.

A rich text editor provided by SharePoint Services allows you to create HTML pages without having to write any HTML code. Users with no coding experience can easily add formatted web pages to the team site.

Web Parts in SharePoint Services can also communicate with each other. This powerful feature allows you to create a Web Part that provides the data for another Web Part on your team site without having to write intricate code.

You can also build complex Web Part pages that can display several unrelated pieces of information on one page. By displaying several Web Parts on one page, users no longer have to navigate to multiple pages or web sites to retrieve information.

In this chapter you will learn:

- How to link external content to your team site, including HTML pages, system folders, and files
- How to create static HTML pages without writing cumbersome HTML code
- The benefit of connecting Web Parts to allow your Web Parts to produce or consume information from other Web Parts
- The benefits of creating custom Web Parts that extend the functionality of the standard Web Parts offered by SharePoint Services

By the end of this chapter, you should understand the benefits and methods of linking external content to your SharePoint team sites.

Linking to External Content

Windows SharePoint Services includes Web Parts that allow you to link to external content such as documents, shared folders, and web sites that aren't part of the actual team site. By adding a Page Viewer Web Part to your team site, you can display external files, folders, or web sites to users in a transparent fashion. In other words, you can extend the reach of your team site in order to present content that is not under your direct control.

Adding a Page Viewer Web Part

A Page Viewer Web Part provides a window for displaying external content on a shared page. For example, you could link to a stock ticker, or an important spreadsheet that contains all product codes that users need to create invoices. In either case, the content is not under your direct control, so you can't simply add it to a standard Web Part. Figure 3-1 shows how you browse the Web Part list to add Web Parts to your team site.

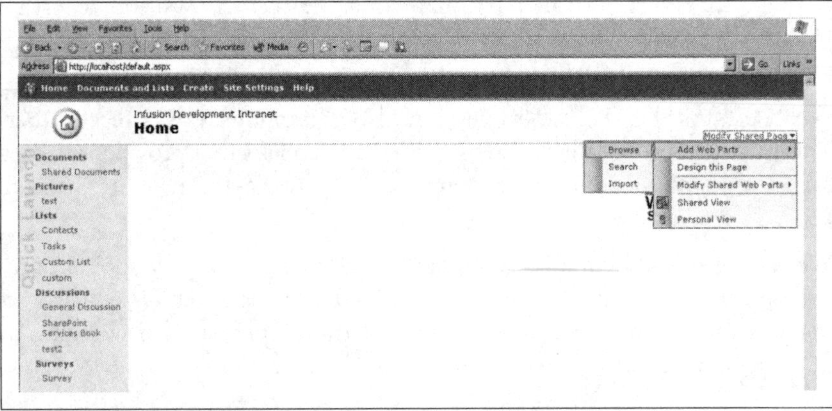

Figure 3-1. Browsing the Web Part list

To add a Page Viewer Web Part:

1. Click on the "Modify Shared page" link in the top-right corner of the page.
2. Select Add Web Parts → Browse.
3. Select the Page Viewer Web Part from the list.
4. Select Left or Right from the Add to drop-down list to add your part to the lefthand or righthand side of the page.
5. Click OK.

Personalizing a Page Viewer Web Part

SharePoint Services Web Parts support personalization. That is, each user can configure his view of a site. As the site designer, you can configure a Page Viewer Web Part in the Page Viewer Web Part configuration menu to allow a user to specify how the Web Part appears on the page. Many of the properties are style choices, but some options are worth noting.

- Set the height and width properties for the Web Part:
  - To ensure the Web Part is always the same size, set the properties to a fixed pixel size. The user will not be able to adjust the size of the part.
  - To allow the window size to change depending on the content being displayed, select the "Adjust to fit zone" radio button.
- To display the Page Viewer Web Part on the page, select the Visible checkbox.
- To determine where the Web Part is displayed (that is, the order) on your page, enter a numeric value in the Part Order text field. If you enter a `1`, the Page Viewer Web Part will be displayed as the first item in its area. If you don't enter a value, the user will be able to adjust the Web Part order.
- If you want the user to have the option to minimize the Page Viewer Web Part, select the "Allow Minimize" checkbox.
- If you want the user to be able to close the Page Viewer Web Part, select the "Allow Close" checkbox. If this checkbox is not selected, the Page Viewer Web Part will always be displayed.
- If you want the user to be able to change the location of the Page Viewer Web Part, select the "Allow Move" checkbox.

Linking to a web site

Linking a Page Viewer Web Part to an external web page allows you to display the information from any web site in a frame contained on your page. For example, your site could link to a web site that displayed a news ticker, weather updates, or stock information. To link to a web site:

1. Click "Open tool pane" in the Page Viewer Web Part.
2. In the Page Viewer menu, select the Web Page radio button.
3. Type the URL of the web site you want to display in the Link text field. To test if the link you entered is valid, click on the Test Link hyperlink. If the hyperlink is valid, the web site is loaded into a pop-up viewer window. If

the hyperlink is invalid, the pop-up viewer displays a Page Not Found error page.

4. Type a title for your Web Part in the Title text field.
5. Configure the appearance and layout of your Page Viewer Web Part.

Figure 3-2 shows the configuration options that are available when you create a Page Viewer Web Part.

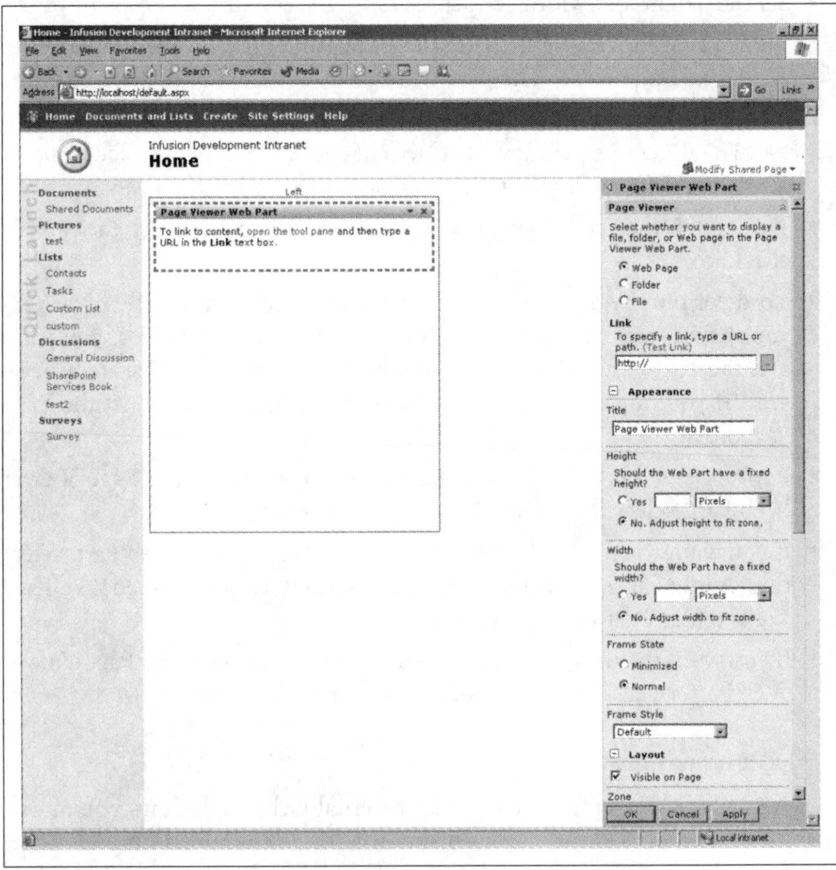

Figure 3-2. Creating a part viewer Web Part

Linking to a folder

If you link a Page Viewer Web Part to a system folder, your users will be able to view any documents or subfolders stored in the parent folder. For example, you might want to link to a folder containing corporate standards documents. The documents are not under the control of your group, so you wouldn't want to put them in a document library Web Part. However, you need to have access to the files. A Page Viewer Web Part is the perfect choice for this scenario because it provides seamless access to the files without granting editing rights. To link to a folder:

1. Click "Open tool pane" in the Page Viewer Web Part.
2. In the Page Viewer menu, select the Folder radio button.
3. In the Link text field, type the path to the folder you want to display (for example, **`C:\InetPub`**).
4. Configure the appearance and layout of your Page Viewer Web Part.

Linking to a file

You can also use a Page Viewer Web Part to display a specific file. For example, you could add a Page Viewer Web Part to the employee timesheet page, so that each time a user fills out a weekly timesheet he can see a file displaying all of the valid project numbers. To link to a file:

1. Click "Open tool pane" in the Page Viewer Web Part.
2. In the Page Viewer menu, select the File radio button.
3. Click Browse and navigate to the file you want to display.
4. Configure the appearance and layout of your Page Viewer Web Part.

Figure 3-3 displays a page that contains three Page Viewer Web Parts. The first Page Viewer Web Part (1) is called "Web Page" and is linked to the CodeNotes web site. The second Page Viewer Web Part (2) is called "Folder" and is linked to the *C:\InetPub* folder. The final Page Viewer Web Part (3) is called "File" and is linked to an XML file.

Notice that each of the Page Viewer Web Parts displays a different style of content. The Web Page Viewer (1) displays the web page as you'd see it inside of Internet Explorer, whereas the Folder Page Viewer (2) displays a view reminiscent of a Windows Explorer tab.

Creating HTML Pages

From time to time, you may need to create a static web page on your team site. Although you could create the page externally and link to it with a Page Viewer Web Part, you can also take advantage of the built-in HTML features of SharePoint Services. You can create a page by adding text, pictures, and tables through your web browser without writing any HTML code. By default, all of the web pages you create are stored in the shared documents library.

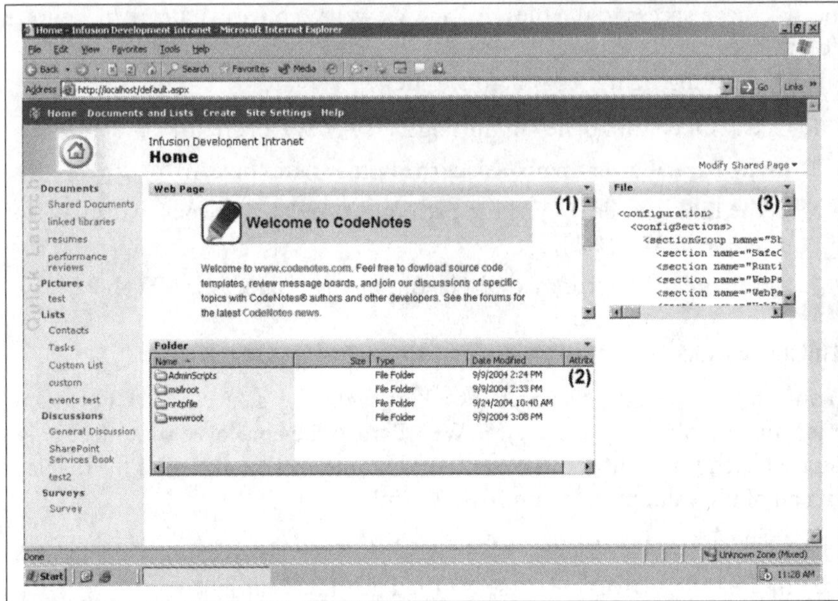

Figure 3-3. Page Viewer Web Parts

To create an HTML page in SharePoint Services:

1. Click Create in the top menu bar located at the top of the page.
2. Click Basic Web Page to open up the New Basic Page form.

Figure 3-4 shows the New Basic Page, which is used to create new HTML pages for your team site:

1. Type a name for your web page in the Name text field. Note that your page is always given the extension *.aspx* even though the page only contains basic HTML.
2. If you want to overwrite an existing file with the same name, select the "Overwrite if file already exists?" checkbox.
3. Select where you want to save the web page from the Document Library drop-down list.
4. Click Create.

Figure 3-5 shows the Rich Text Editor – Web Page Dialog box that is launched after you click the Create button. You can use the Web Page Dialog box to create simple *.aspx* pages without writing tedious HTML code. You can add and format text, insert images, and create tables and lists just as you would in Microsoft Word.

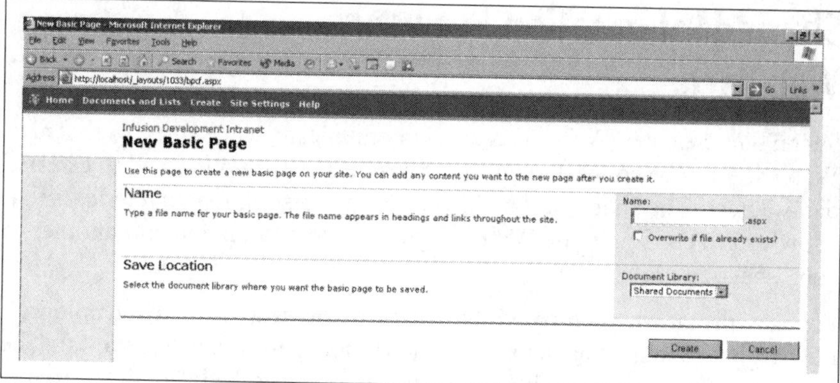

Figure 3-4. Create basic web page form

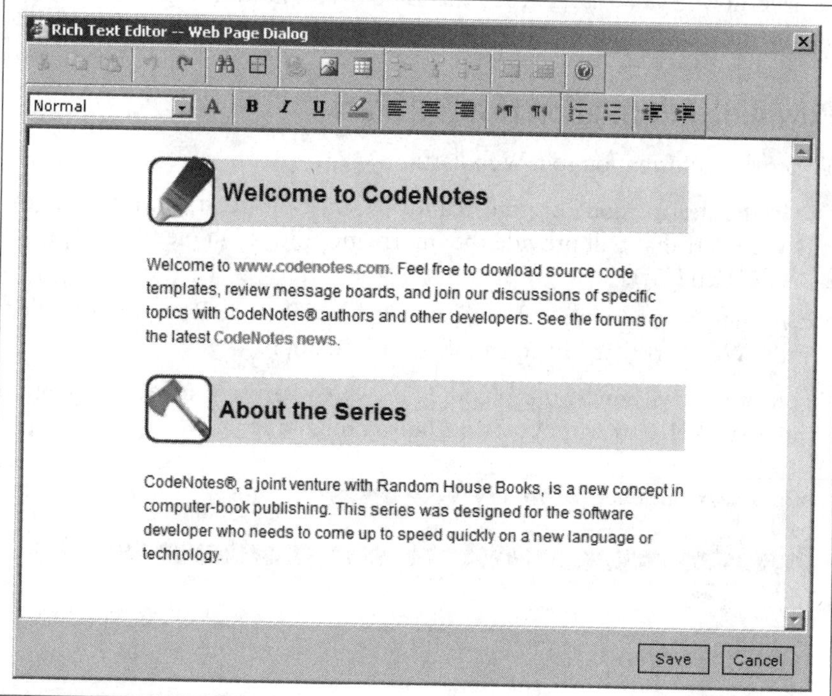

Figure 3-5. Web Page Dialog box

Sharing Information Between Web Parts

SharePoint Services Web Parts can communicate with other Web Parts. Web Parts can be connected and synchronized to each other and to external data sources. The SharePoint architecture supports *connection interfaces* that allow you to configure one Web Part to provide information and another to consume it.

For example, at your company's human resources team site, each employee's file might contain the scheduled dates for performance reviews. The Employee File document library would pass the scheduled dates to the announcement Web Part. The announcement list would automatically retrieve new review dates from the Employee File document library and update itself accordingly.

Providing Information to a Web Part

To provide information to a Web Part:

1. In the design mode of your team site, click on the down arrow of the Web Part that will provide the information (for example, the Employee File Web Part).
2. In the pop-up menu, select Connections → Provide Row To and select the Web Part that will consume the information.

Figure 3-6 shows how you can configure a Web Part to provide information to another Web Part without writing any configuration code.

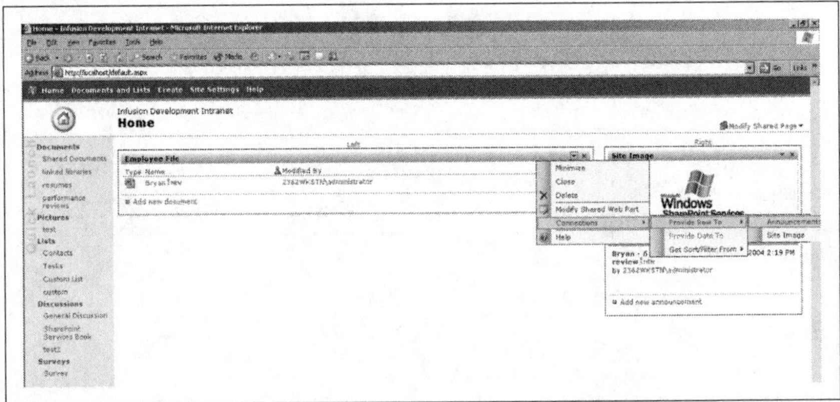

Figure 3-6. Configuring the Employee File Web Part to provide information to the Announcements Web Part

The actual code that sends and receives events is beyond the scope of this book. However, you can work with your developers to create custom Web Parts that provide additional communication options within your Windows SharePoint Services sites.

The Employee File Web Part will now broadcast information to the announcements Web Part.

Consuming Information from a Web Part

Not only do you have to establish the link from the provider Web Part (the Employee File) to the consuming Web Part (the announcements list), you also have to tell the consumer Web Part how to use the information. In this example, you want the announcements list to display a new row based on the data sent by the Employee File Web Part.

To consume information from a Web Part:

1. In the design mode, click on the down arrow of the Web Part that will consume the information (for example, the Announcements Web Part).
2. In the resulting menu, select Connections → Get Sort/Filter From and select the Web Part that will provide the information (for example, the Employee File Web Part).

Figure 3-7 shows how you can configure a Web Part to consume information from another Web Part without writing any configuration code.

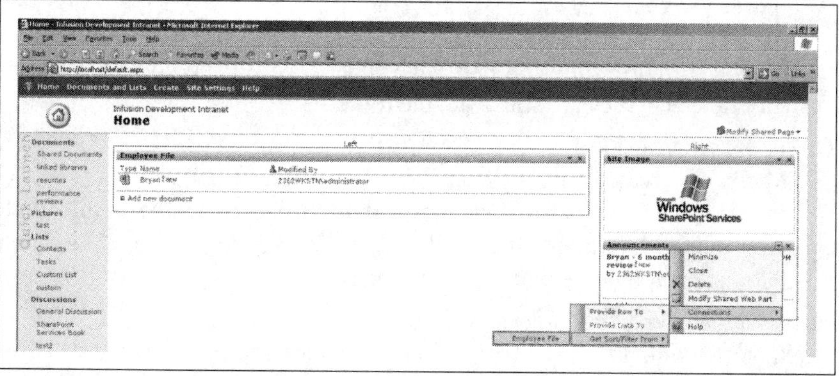

Figure 3-7. Configuring the announcements Web Part to consume information from the Employee File Web Part

Custom Web Part Pages

Although you can combine individual Web Parts into a site, you may want to group individual Web Parts into a complex Web Part page. By implementing a Web Part page, you can display lists, charts, text, and images as a single Web Part component. Organizing related data and web pages eliminates the time and steps required for users to constantly access multiple web pages and data sources. For example, you can build a custom Web Part page that displays a customer's contact information, orders, and invoices. All three pieces of information will be grouped as a single Web Part control.

Web Part pages can be used to:

- Combine data from multiple data sources
- Report data (e.g., aggregate data or prioritized data)
- Access any external sites that users require in daily tasks
- Display updated schedules and meeting information

Web Part Galleries

Any Web Parts that are available for you to add to your SharePoint Services team site are stored in Web Part galleries. Depending on how your site is configured, Web Parts can be stored in any of four galleries:

Site Web Part gallery
: Any site-level Web Part made available by the server administrator is stored in the Site Web Part gallery.

Web Part Page gallery
: Any Web Part that is available to a page, but not visible on a Web Part page is stored in the Web Part Page gallery. When a Web Part is closed (not deleted), they are still available to a user.

Online Web Part gallery
: Microsoft created several Web Parts (for example, MSNBC stock tickers, weather, and news Web Parts) that are stored in the online Web Part gallery. Eventually, the Online Web Part gallery will include Web Parts created by other software vendors.

Virtual Server Web Part gallery
: If your company has several sites, it makes sense to store any commonly used Web Parts in one centralized location. The Virtual Server Web Part gallery stores any Web Parts that can be used across multiple sites.

Creating a Custom Web Part Page

The easiest way to create a custom Web Part page is through the New Web Part Page form. After creating a page with the New Web Part page form, you can easily design the page in a web browser.

To create a new custom Web Part page:

1. Click Create in the top menu bar located at the top of the page.
2. Under Web Pages, click Web Part Page to open the New Web Part Page dialog.

Figure 3-8 shows the New Web Part Page screen that you can use to create new Web Part pages and choose the template that your Web Part page uses:

1. In the dialog, type a name for your Web Part page in the Name text field. Once again, your custom page will always have an *.aspx* extension.
2. If you want the new page to overwrite existing files with the same name, select the "Overwrite if file exists?" checkbox.
3. Select the layout you want for your Web Part page from the Layout Template list box. The template determines the graphical layout of your Web Part (for example, whether the Web Part has a header or footer, and the number of columns displayed to the user). Figure 3-9 displays the "Header, Left Column, Body" template.
4. Select a location to save your new Web Part page from the Document Library drop-down list. You have to save all custom Web Part pages in a valid document library.
5. Click Create.

After you click the Create button, your newly created Web Part page opens in the design view. Figure 3-9 shows a Web Part page in design view. Depending on the layout you chose, you will have several Web Part zones in which you can drag and drop existing Web Parts from the Web Part list. The Web Part page has three Web Part zones (a header, a left column, and a body zone).

For example, you could drag and drop an image Web Part into the header zone to add a company's logo to your page. You could then add custom lists to the left column and

Modifying Your Web Parts Page in an HTML Editor

Most Web Part page properties can be accessed and modified directly through a web browser. In some cases you may want to make advanced modifications to your Web Parts page. Web Parts pages are stored as ASP.

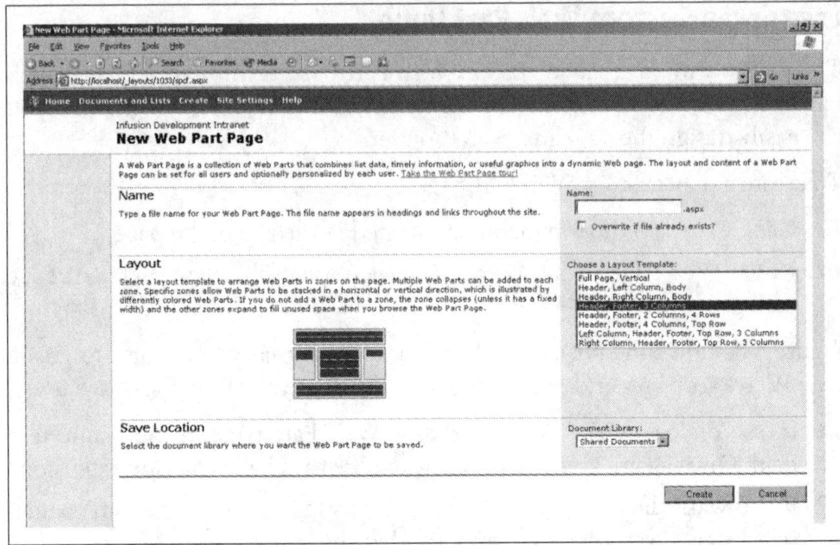

Figure 3-8. Create a custom Web Part Page

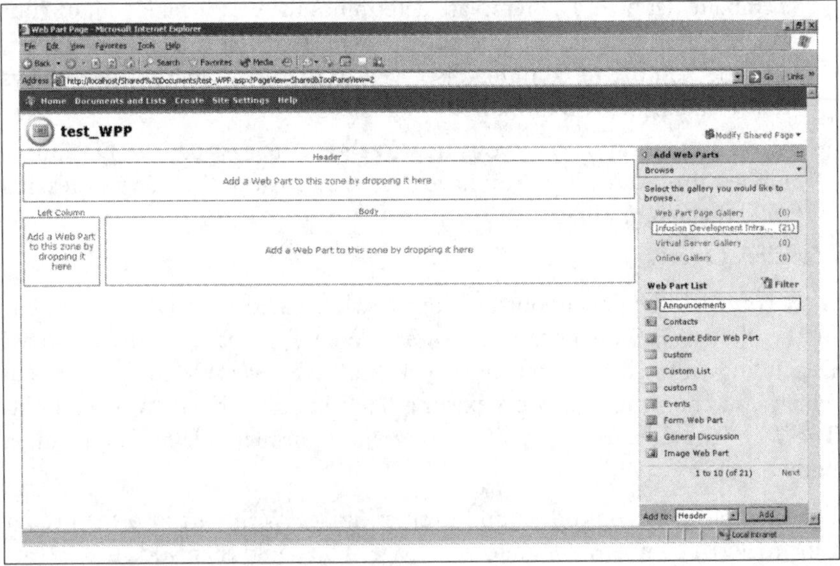

Figure 3-9. Web Part page design view

NET (*.aspx*) files. Therefore, you can modify Web Parts pages with an HTML editor such as Microsoft FrontPage. Figure 3-10 shows a Web Part page opened in FrontPage. Using FrontPage to edit your SharePoint Services team site gives you more control over the information you choose to display, as well as how you display it. For example, you can:

- Modify the theme of a Web Part page
- Modify the Web Part template
- Modify zone properties
- Add or edit HTML code
- Create customized data views from XML or database sources

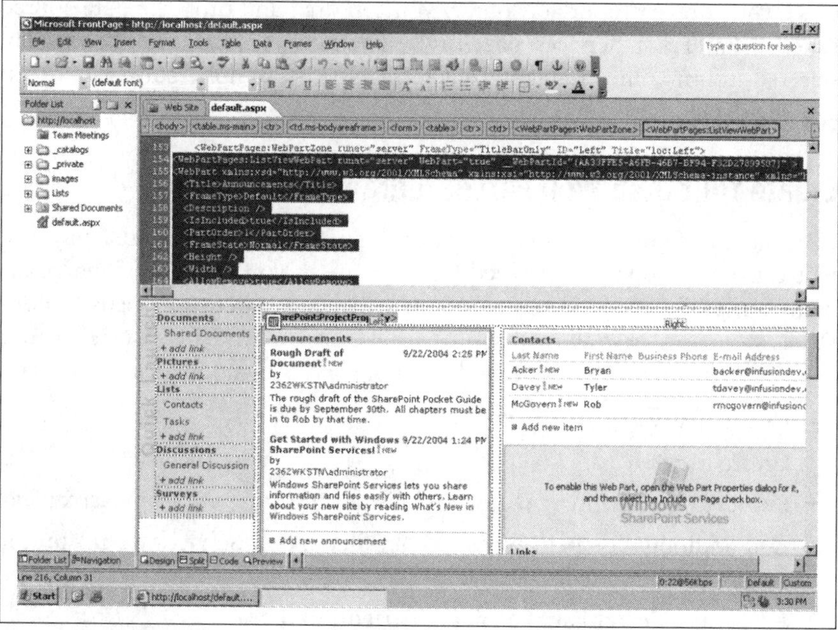

Figure 3-10. Opening a Web Part in FrontPage

You can also add web controls (for example, counters, navigation controls, and applets) that cannot be added through the basic SharePoint Services web interface. To add a control to your page:

1. Open the page in Microsoft FrontPage 2003 by selecting File → Open and navigating to your page.
2. Insert a web component on your page by selecting Insert → Web Component.
3. Select the type of component you want to add to your page. You can insert any valid web component type, including applets, counters, or additional navigation.
4. Save your page.

Once you have edited a page outside of WSS, any changes should automatically appear when you refresh your view of the site.

Creating customized data views

Implementing the data view Web Part allows you create customized data views by connecting to any data source that generates XML (for example, SQL Server, XML files, XML web services, and standard SharePoint Services lists).

Once you connect to a data source, you can drag and drop the data source onto a SharePoint Services page and customize the data view to display selected information in customized formats (for example, adding borders, filtering data, and sorting).

Create Your Own Web Parts Programmatically

In some cases, the functionality offered by existing Web Parts may not match the functionality you need for your site. If you use a design environment compatible with SharePoint Services such as Microsoft Visual Studio .NET, you can access all the features available to ASP.NET to create custom Web Parts that match your desired functionality. Programmatically you can:

- Define new views
- Create forms
- Retrieve database information and display information on an .aspx page
- Add additional content types to your SharePoint Services team site (for example, Macromedia Flash movies)
- Add Active Server Pages (ASP.NET pages) to the site

The steps involved in creating a custom Web Part are beyond the scope of this book.

CHAPTER 4

Securing SharePoint Sites

Every SharePoint site needs security to ensure users are limited to performing just the tasks they ought to be performing. You would not want an unauthorized employee viewing the Human Resources files, nor would you want a nonemployee accessing certain corporate documents. Security policies dictate user access, user rights, and user permissions. Windows SharePoint Services incorporates a flexible and dynamic security model that allows administrators and users to control access to their pages with ease.

In this chapter, you will learn how Windows SharePoint Services authenticates users and grants permissions. This chapter provides detailed steps and overviews on:

- User and site group management
- Security architecture
- Assigning roles to objects and sites

Once you have completed this chapter, you should understand how to secure a SharePoint team site.

Users and Site Groups

Users access SharePoint sites to add, view, edit, and delete content. To ensure users retrieve the appropriate content, Windows SharePoint Services provides you with a flexible security model. Whenever you work with security, you have to consider two separate but equally important processes:

Authentication
: The process of authentication determines whether a user is who he says he is. Authentication generally involves comparing a username and password to a set of stored *credentials*. The credentials prove that the user accessing your site is a legitimate user.

Authorization

Once you have authenticated a user, the next step is to decide which resources the user can access. This process is known as authorization. In most cases, configuring authorization requires that a site administrator map a user to a *permission set*.

Windows SharePoint Services supports authentication through easily configurable integration with Windows Server 2003, Active Directory, and Microsoft Internet Information Services (IIS). Authorization, on the other hand, requires that you create *site groups* (permission sets) linked to one or more users. A site group is assigned to a user when the user initially accesses the site. You can also change the site group a user belongs to through SharePoint's site settings. This process is outlined in the section "Site Group Management" later in this chapter.

User Management

Windows SharePoint Services simplifies user management by relying on IIS and Microsoft Windows Server 2003 to manage user accounts and authentication. Either Windows Server 2003 or Active Directory can be used to manage the user accounts; however, IIS is always used to manage user authentication.

User Account Modes

Windows SharePoint Services provides two user administration modes:

- Domain account mode
- Active Directory account creation mode

When you or your administrator installs and configures Windows SharePoint Services on a department or company server (see Chapter 6 for more information on installing Windows SharePoint Services), you choose the account mode to use in SharePoint. This is an important decision—once you select one mode, you cannot change back to the other mode without uninstalling and reinstalling Windows SharePoint Services. Further, SharePoint will not run in a mixed mode.

A default Windows SharePoint Services installation uses domain account mode. Domain account mode allows users with Windows Domain accounts access to your site. This account mode is best suited when you plan to use SharePoint internally on a Windows-based network where your systems administrator controls user creation.

If you plan to use SharePoint externally, choose Active Directory account creation mode. In Active Directory account creation mode, you can create users in the SharePoint central administration web site. SharePoint then adds the user to Active Directory after creation.

Authentication Modes

SharePoint limits which users can access a team site through authentication. Granting a user access to a site means the user passed authentication. Denying a user access to a site means the user failed authentication. Windows SharePoint Services uses IIS to control how a user is authenticated. IIS provides four authentication methods (in order of increasing security):

Anonymous authentication
: This mode grants all users access to a SharePoint site. Anonymous access contains no advance security features. You should restrict the use of this mode to external SharePoint sites while securing all internal documents against access from anonymous users.

Basic authentication
: More secure than anonymous authentication, basic authentication requires all users to provide credentials prior to accessing the site. However, transmitting the credentials poses a security risk. Credentials are passed along the network in clear text, with no encryption provided. Like anonymous access, use of this authentication mode should be restricted.

Integrated Windows authentication
: This is the default authentication mode. A user provides her Windows domain account to access a SharePoint site. If a user does not have a Windows domain account, IIS prompts the user to enter a username and password.

Certificates authentication
: Certificates authentication uses SSL certificates to authenticate a user. To implement this mode, you need to configure both IIS and Windows SharePoint Services to accept certificates, which must be generated by a certificate authority such as Verisign or Thwate.

You can choose any of the four authentication methods, depending on the security needs for your site.

Default User Permissions

After authenticating a user, SharePoint assigns a default set of permissions to the user. By default, new users receive the site group *reader* (see the section

"Site Group Management"). You can change this setting and grant increased access rights or even grant administrative rights. You can also create different sets of rites for different users or user groups.

Site Group Management

Site groups allow you to grant roles to users and groups. You can think of a site group as a set of permissions that restrict what tasks a user can and cannot perform within your SharePoint site. As a site administrator, you can create specific site groups for specific users and functions. Once you have your site group created, you can link it to either a specific user or a specific group.

Default Site Groups

SharePoint installs five default site groups that you can apply in most situations. Each of the default groups allows different permissions that are useful for different types of users. However, if the default groups do not suit your needs, you can also create custom groups.

Guest

The guest site group provides the lowest possible permission level to users without denying site access. This group restricts users and user groups to read-only access. You should use this site group for default users and groups that are not assigned to a site group with greater access rights.

Reader

The reader site group has more access than the guest site group. A reader has permission to:

- Read all content in the site.
- Create a new site using the "Self-Service Site Creation" option. Self-service site creation allows a user to create a new top-level site. When a user creates a new site, he becomes the administrator of that site but still maintains his existing site groups for other areas in SharePoint.

A user assigned to the reader site group cannot make modifications to content on the site. You assign this site group to users and groups who need access to content on the site but do not need to modify the content.

Contributor

The contributor site group inherits the reader site group permissions, plus the ability to:

- Add, modify, and delete content in existing document libraries and lists
- Manage personal views
- Add and remove personal Web Parts
- Create cross-site groups

A contributor cannot create a document library; however, he can add content to, delete content from, or modify content on an existing library.

You should assign this site group to users and groups who need full control over content in document libraries and lists.

Web designer

The web designer site group inherits the contributor site group permissions, plus the ability to:

- Manage lists and document libraries
- Create and modify web pages
- Manage themes and borders
- Apply style sheets to the site

The web designer site group provides advanced control over a SharePoint site, without granting full administrative control. You should assign this site group to users and groups who are taking ownership of a SharePoint site. Keep in mind that a user in the web designer group does not have full administrative control, although she does have great power over how the site is organized and maintained.

Administrator

The final default site group, administrator, inherits the web designer site group permissions, plus the ability to:

- Manage groups for the site
- Create sites
- Create workspace sites
- Manage list permissions
- View usage analysis data

You cannot delete or customize the administrator site group, and one user must always be assigned to this group. You should only grant this permission type to users who are going to control access to sites. Generally, this role is reserved for system administrators and other users who have full trust within an organization. Most users do not need any rights higher than the web designer group.

Automatically Assigning a User to a Site Group

By default, SharePoint assigns users to site groups. To change the default site group that the user receives, modify the Anonymous Access settings on the Site Settings screen. To modify these settings, follow the following steps:

1. Click Site Settings at the top of the screen.
2. Click on the link Go to Site Administration under the heading Administration.
3. Click on the link Manage Anonymous Access under the heading Users and Permissions.
4. Under the section All Authenticated Users, you can change the drop-down list to a new default site group.

Figure 4-1 shows the Change Anonymous Access Settings page, which is used to assign users to specific site groups and to determine what access anonymous users are granted.

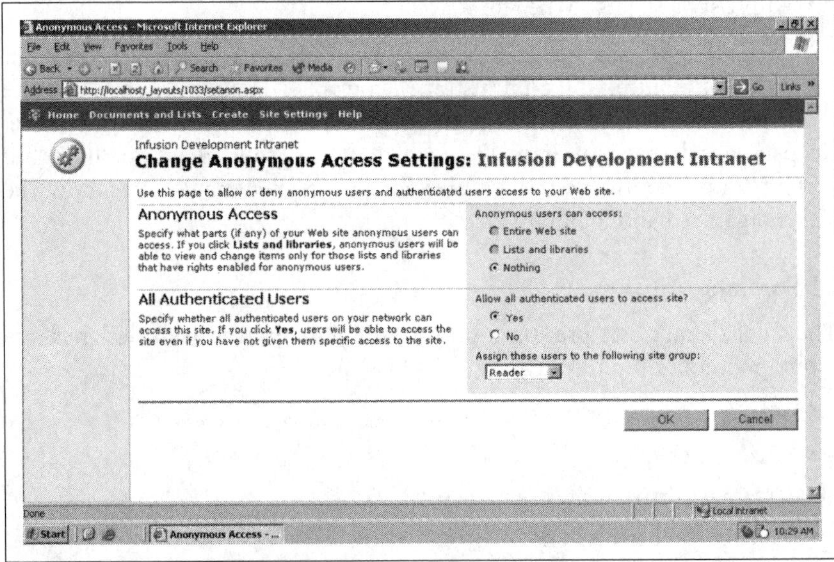

Figure 4-1. Default site group assignment

You can change a user's site group assignment. Site groups are assigned at three levels:

- Global
- Site
- Object

The section "Security Architecture" discusses these topics in detail.

Managing Site Groups

The default site groups do not solve every situation. To provide maximum flexibility, Windows SharePoint Services lets you to create, modify, and delete site groups. By allowing customization of site groups, SharePoint allows you to create a flexible security architecture that adapts to your business requirements.

Site group conflicts

You can assign multiple site groups to a user. If two site groups conflict, the site group that applies to the immediate content being viewed is applied. For instance, you could assign a user to the reader site group for the corporate Human Resources SharePoint team site, the web designer site group for the Training SharePoint team site, and the contributor site group everywhere else. In this scenario, when a user accesses the Human Resources site, two site groups conflict: reader and contributor. Because the user is viewing the Human Resources site (the most immediate content), he will have reader access and the contributor site group will not be valid.

Security Architecture

In order to understand how site groups and user assignments work together to provide full security, you must understand the overall security architecture built into Web Parts and Windows SharePoint Services.

Windows SharePoint Services handles security in order of priority:

- Use object-level permissions, if they exist.
- Use site-level permissions if no object-level permissions exist.
- Use global-level permissions if no other permissions exist.

SharePoint assigns global permissions when a user enters SharePoint for the first time. Users receive site-level permissions when they access a site. Generally, a user who doesn't belong to the administrative group receives reader permissions when he accesses a SharePoint site.

Site-Level Permissions

The amount of site access a user requires depends on the tasks the user needs to perform. For example, if a user needs to add content to the team site, she requires the appropriate access rights to do so. To grant these permissions, you need to assign users to a site group to control site access.

Controlling site access

Each site in SharePoint maintains its own permissions for users. You can manage user permissions through the Site Administration page on the team site. From this page, you can:

Manage users
: Add and delete users and control a user's access to the site.

Manage site groups
: Add, delete, and modify the permissions available to a site group.

Manage anonymous access
: Enable or disable anonymous access and decide the default site group to which users should be assigned.

Manage cross-site groups
: Add, modify, and delete cross-site groups.

Manage access request
: Allow users to send requests for access to functionality within a site to which they are denied.

Assigning a user to a site group

To assign a user to a site group permission set for a site, you need to:

1. Click the Site Settings link on the top menu bar.
2. Select Manage Users.
3. Click on the user to modify access rights for the selected user.
4. Click the checkbox associated with the site group to assign the user to that group.
5. Click OK.

Figure 4-2 shows the Edit Site Group Membership page for a team site.

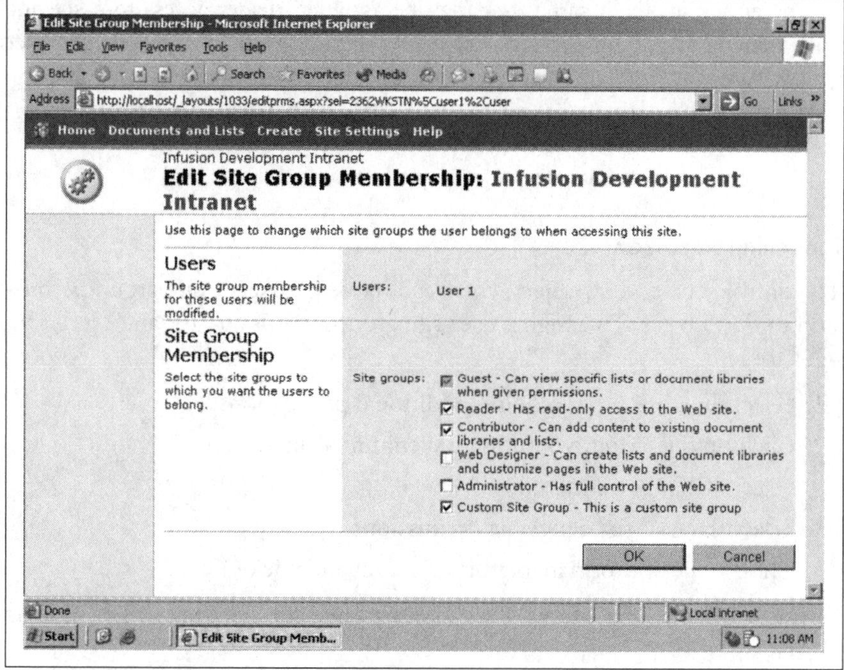

Figure 4-2. Team site permission screen

You can assign more than one site group to a user for a site. This is useful when you have site groups that do not inherit permissions (for example, a read-only site group, an add-only site group, and a delete-only site group).

Object-Level Permissions

Site-level permissions handle many of your security requirements. However, a user may require different access rights to specific content within a site. To increase the flexibility of the security model, Windows SharePoint Services allows you to assign object-level permissions.

Object-level permissions exist for all objects. You can configure permissions for:

- Document libraries
- Picture libraries
- Lists
- Discussion boards
- Surveys

Object-level permissions permit a more flexible and dynamic layer of security for users and groups. Whereas a user may require the web designer permission for the entire site, that same user may be assigned reader access to a specific document library. The user can do everything allowed by the web designer group; however, once the user accesses the document library in the site, the user is restricted to the rights that apply to the reader role. This sort of scenario is quite common when you have a site developer supporting a sensitive team site (such as a financial information site or human resources site).

Controlling object access

To control access to an object, you need to assign users a site group permission to that object. To assign a user site group permission for an object, you need to:

1. Select the object that requires additional permissions.
2. Click on the "Modify settings and columns" link.
3. Select "Change permissions."
4. Select the user to change his permissions.
5. Choose the appropriate permission level and click OK.

Figure 4-3 shows the Modify Permissions page for the Shared Documents object.

Denying user access to an object

To prevent a user access to an object, perform the following steps on the Change Permissions screen:

1. Click on the checkbox beside each user you wish to remove.
2. Click Remove Selected Users.

Removing a user from an object only affects the user's ability to access that particular object. The user's site access permissions are not affected. You might, for example, grant the web developer role for a user who helps administer the Human Resources team site, but you might block his access to the Employee Evaluation document library.

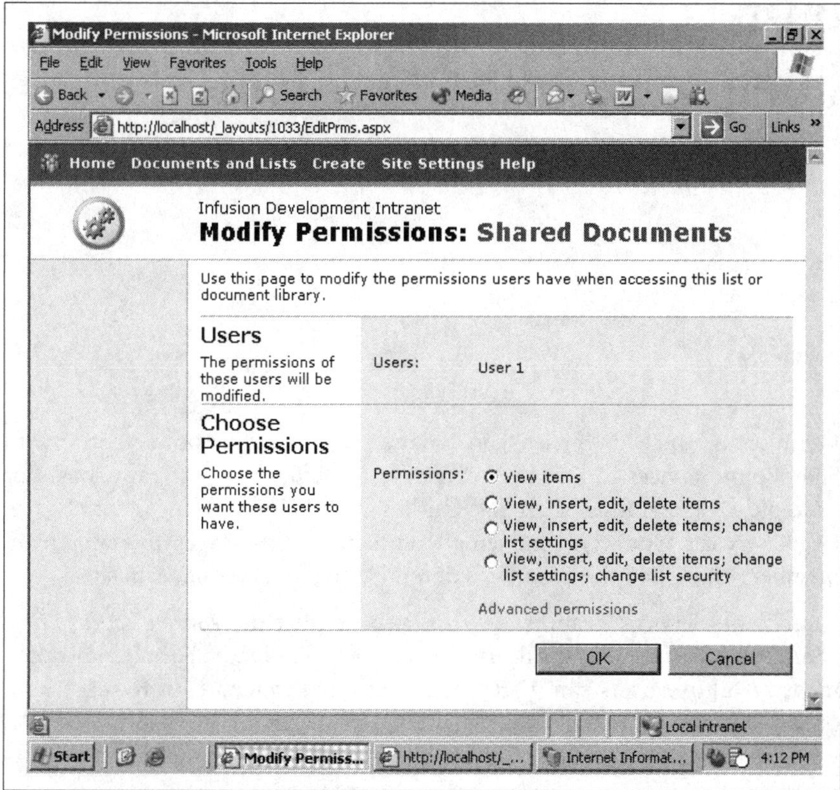

Figure 4-3. Modify Permissions screen

CHAPTER 5

Integrating with Office 2003

If you're an Office 2003 user, you can integrate many of your activities with SharePoint Services to add even more functionality to your team sites. For example, by integrating Microsoft Outlook and MSN Messenger with SharePoint Services, you can send emails and instant messages to other team members and schedule meetings without having to leave the team site.

SharePoint Services team sites can also implement *shared workspaces*. Shared workspaces allow site users to work collaboratively on team documents. Multiple users can work collaboratively to prepare an Excel, Word, or PowerPoint document while ensuring that changes are monitored and versioned.

SharePoint Services team sites also support XML-based forms. By integrating SharePoint Services with any compatible XML editor (such as Microsoft InfoPath) you can import or create forms to retrieve input from site users. By combining all of these integrations, you can greatly increase the abilities of a team site.

In this chapter, you will learn how to:

- Integrate SharePoint Services with Microsoft Office 2003
- Configure an online presence so you and members of your team can send real-time messages to other team members currently logged into the team site
- Create and use shared workspaces
- Create and use meeting workspaces
- Create and use forms in a form library

By the end of this chapter, you should understand the benefits of integrating SharePoint Services with Microsoft Office 2003.

Finding Out Who's Online

By integrating SharePoint Services with Microsoft Active Directory, Microsoft Exchange, and Windows Messenger, you can display user information, including office location, phone extension, and current projects for all your team members. In addition, SharePoint Services implements an online presence indicator that displays whether team site users are online and if they are currently available or busy.

To implement online presence, you must have Microsoft Office 2003 installed and must be running either MSN Messaging or Windows Messenger. Each team user must have a valid Messenger account. When you install Microsoft Office 2003 on your server, an ActiveX control is also installed. The ActiveX control allows SharePoint Services to return online information for all your site users.

By integrating with MSN Messenger or Windows Messenger, users can send instant messages to any site user who is currently online. Figure 5-1 shows the dialog box that allows you to send instant messages to team members.

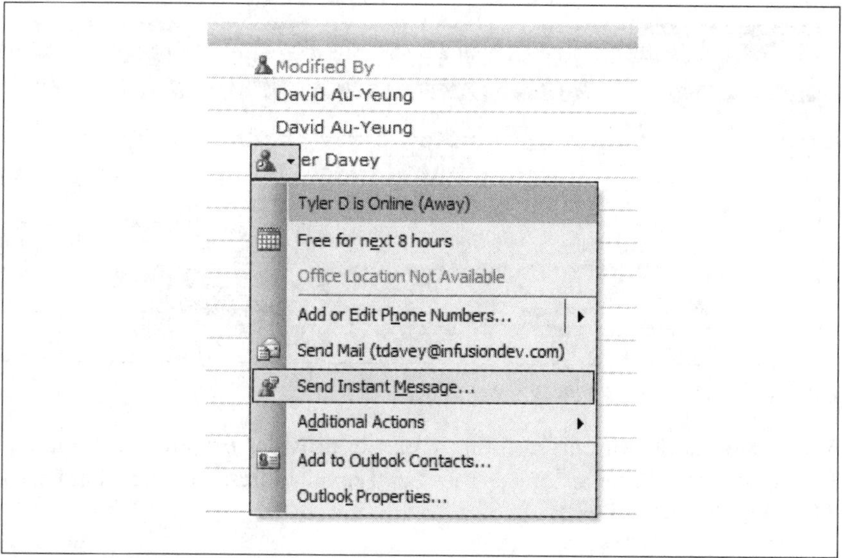

Figure 5-1. Sending an instant message from your team site

For SharePoint to recognize your online presence, your Messenger email address and SharePoint email address must match. Note that your SharePoint email address is actually retrieved from Active Directory.

Configuring Online Presence Information

Before you can use the presence information, you must configure your virtual server to allow online presence. To configure your virtual server:

1. Open the SharePoint Central Administration page by selecting Start → Administrative Tools → SharePoint Central Administration.
2. Click "Configure virtual server settings" in the Virtual Server Configuration section.
3. Click the name of the server you want to configure.
4. Click "Virtual server general settings" in the Virtual Management section.

Figure 5-2 shows the Virtual Server General Settings page. You can configure user online presence on the Virtual Server General Settings page:

1. Select the Yes radio button in the Person Name Smart Tag and Presence Settings section.
2. Click OK.

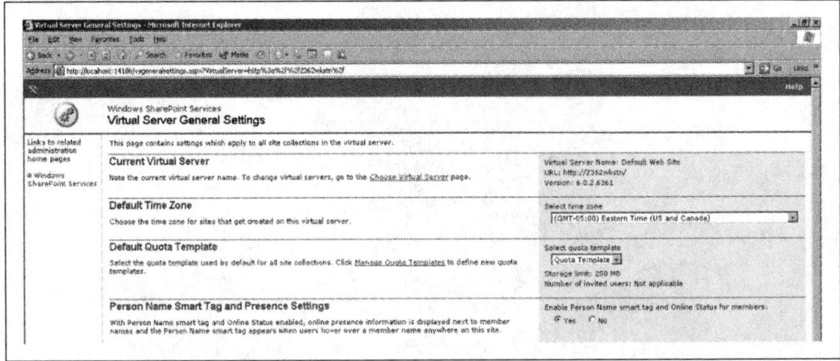

Figure 5-2. Configuring online presence

Windows SharePoint Services automatically provides presence information for any registered user as long as the user's email address matches that user's Messenger email address.

Shared Workspaces

SharePoint Services supports shared workspaces, which allow users to work collaboratively on documents. SharePoint supports two types of shared workspaces:

Document workspaces
: A document workspace site focuses on one or more documents that users can work on collaboratively.

Meeting workspaces
: Meeting workspace sites are used to store all the information and material needed for meetings.

Using Shared Workspaces in Microsoft Office

When you open a shared workspace document in Microsoft Office 2003, the SharePoint Services shared workspace menu is displayed in the Office task pane alongside the document. Integrating the SharePoint shared workspaces menu provides access to all of the SharePoint Services associated with the site where the document is stored without leaving the Office environment.

Figure 5-3 shows a typical Word file opened from a shared workspace. The shared workspace menu (on the righthand side) provides collaboration options made possible by SharePoint Services and shows the online status of all team members.

Other icons provide access to additional features supported by the site, such as a task list or alerts.

The shared workspace menu implements the following SharePoint Web Parts:

Status
: The status Web Part displays any changes in the status of the document.

Document library
: The document library gives a user access to any documents in the shared library.

Links list
: The links list displays any hyperlinks that are available to site users.

Task list
: The task list displays tasks that are assigned to users on the team site. Figure 5-4 shows two tasks linked to a particular document.

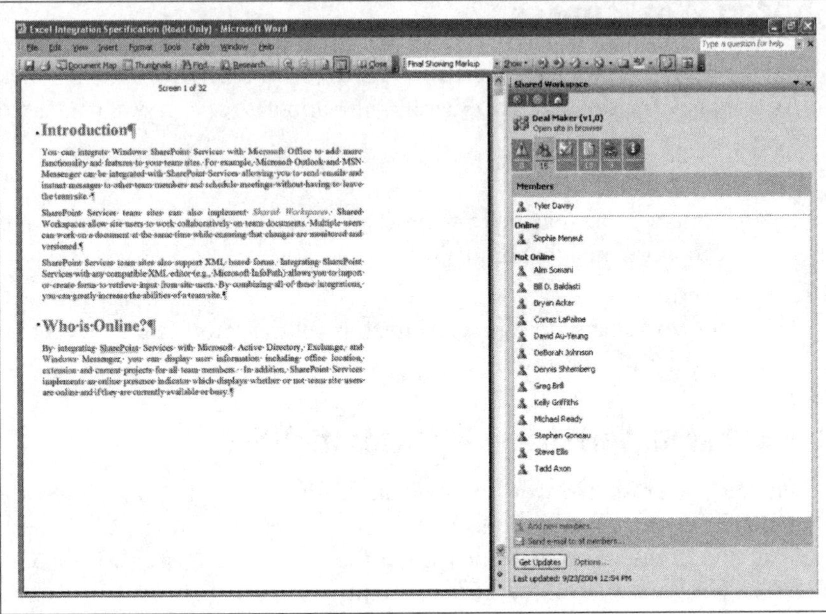

Figure 5-3. Shared workspace

Members

The members Web Part displays a list of all the site members. The members Web Part shows whether or not a user is currently online and allows you to send instant messages and emails to any site member.

Document information

The document information Web Part lists all the document information, including which user created the document, which user last modified the document, and a link to all previous versions of the document.

Configuring Shared Workspace Options

By implementing shared workspaces, you allow more than one user to work on a document at the same time. Therefore, you must configure how a document handles any updates made by users. You can configure the shared workspace to:

- Automatically update the document or workspace
- Always ask a user before performing updates
- Never update the document or workspace when the document is open

You can set the service options by clicking the Options... link at the bottom of the SharePoint shared workspaces menu. Clicking the Options... link

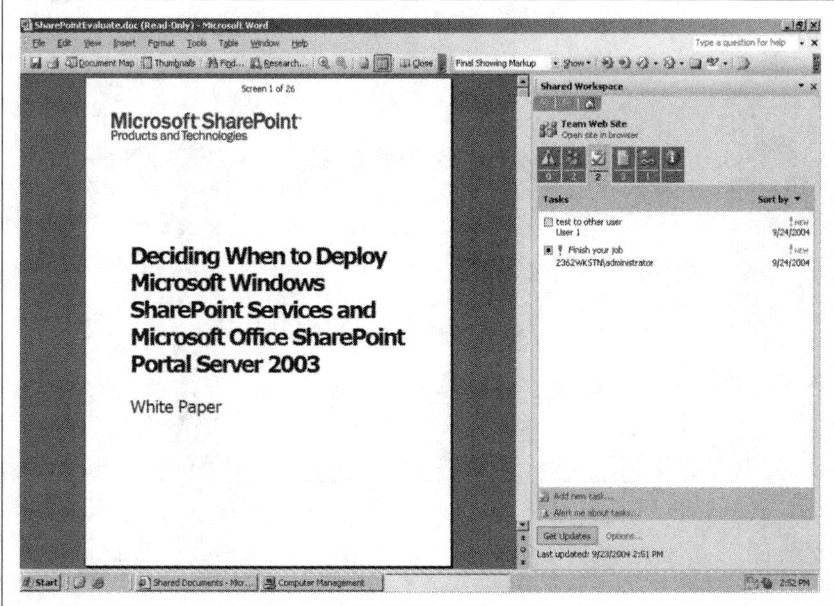

Figure 5-4. Task list in Microsoft Word

launches the Service Options dialog box. The Service Options dialog box is shown in Figure 5-5. To change the settings of the shared workspace:

1. Select Shared Workspace from the Category list.
2. Edit the properties in the dialog box.

For example, you could set up a shared workspace for a business analyst writing a project specification document. By adding the specification document to a shared workspace, other employees working on the project can read the document, record comments, and make changes. The business analyst can then accept or delete any changes and republish the document to the appropriate people.

Document Workspaces

A document workspace site focuses on one or more documents that users can work on collaboratively. Document workspaces support all the features of a basic SharePoint Services team site with the additional functionality of shared workspaces.

The home page of your document workspace site automatically displays the members Web Part. The members Web Part lists all the users who have the proper permissions to use the site. The members Web Part also contains all

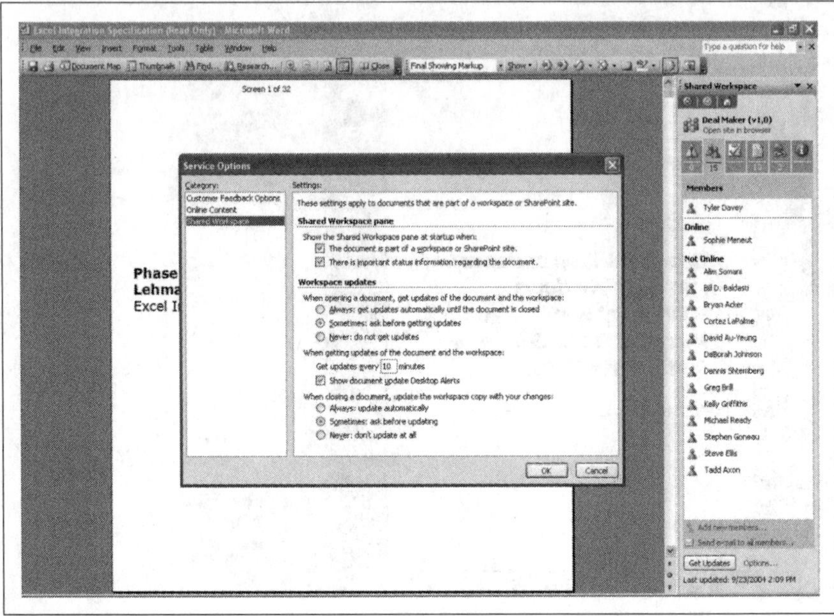

Figure 5-5. Service Options dialog box

the user information for site users, including their online status. You can use the information to send a user an email, book a meeting, or send instant messages to other online team members. Figure 5-6 shows the functionality that the member Web Part offers team members.

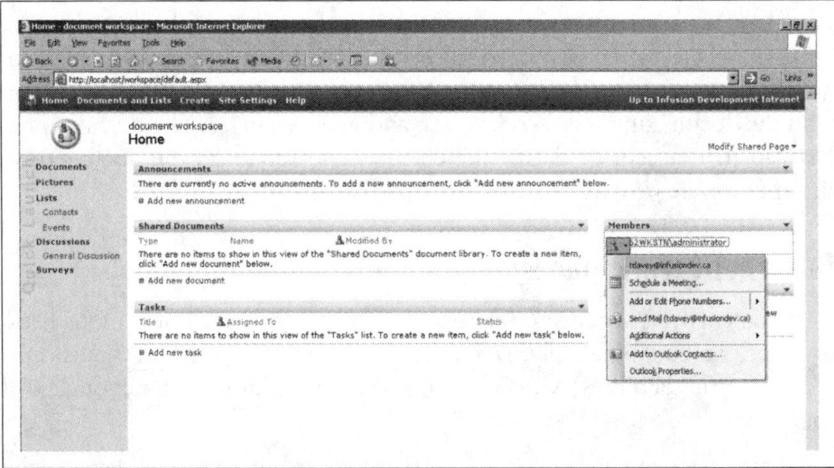

Figure 5-6. Features of the members Web Part

In addition to the members Web Part, you can also configure additional Web Parts relevant to your document space. For example, you can add an announcements list Web Part or a tasks list Web Part so that team members know what needs to be done on any set of documents.

Creating an empty document workspace

Figure 5-7 shows the New SharePoint Site page, which is used to create new SharePoint sites (in this case, a document workspace site). To create an empty document workspace site:

1. Click Create in the top menu bar.
2. Click Sites and Workspaces.
3. Type a title for your new site in the Title text field.
4. Type a brief description of your new site in the Description text area.
5. Enter the URL you want for your document workspace in the URL name field.
6. Select the permissions for your new site by selecting the "Use same permissions as parent site" or "Use unique permissions" radio button.
7. Click Create.
8. In the Template Selection page, select Document Workspace from the Template list box.
9. Click OK.

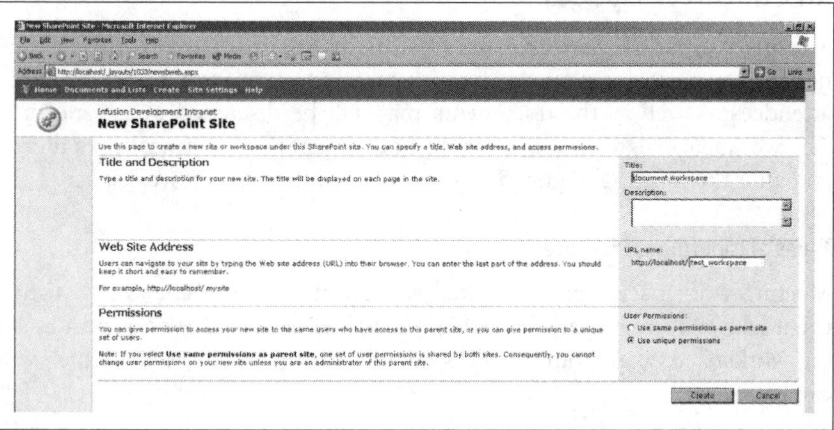

Figure 5-7. New SharePoint Site page

Creating a document workspace for existing documents

To create a document workspace for existing documents:

1. Click Document and Lists in the top menu bar.
2. Select the document library that contains the document.
3. Select the document, and click the Edit arrow.
4. Click Create Document Workspace.

Publishing a document from the document workspace to a document library

If your document is stored in a document library on the team site, you must publish the document back to the original document library once any changes are made in the document workspace. To publish back to the document library:

1. Navigate to the document workspace in a web browser.
2. Click Documents and Lists in your site's top menu bar.
3. Click Document Workspace on the side menu.
4. Click on your desired document workspace.
5. Select the document and click the Edit arrow.
6. Click Publish to Source Location from the menu that appears.

Meeting Workspaces

Meeting workspace sites are used to store all the information and material needed for meetings. You can publish meeting agendas that are sent to all attendees as well as the documents that will be discussed in the meeting. The workspace also allows you to edit documents and to track tasks during and after the meeting. Figure 5-8 shows a standard meeting workspace.

Types of meeting workspaces

Meeting workspaces can be created when you add an event to an existing event list, or through the Create page in SharePoint. When creating a meeting workspace, SharePoint Services includes five templates from which you can choose:

Basic meeting workspace
: The basic meeting workspace template contains all the basic functionality needed to organize and track meetings. The template contains the objective, attendees, and agenda lists Web Parts.

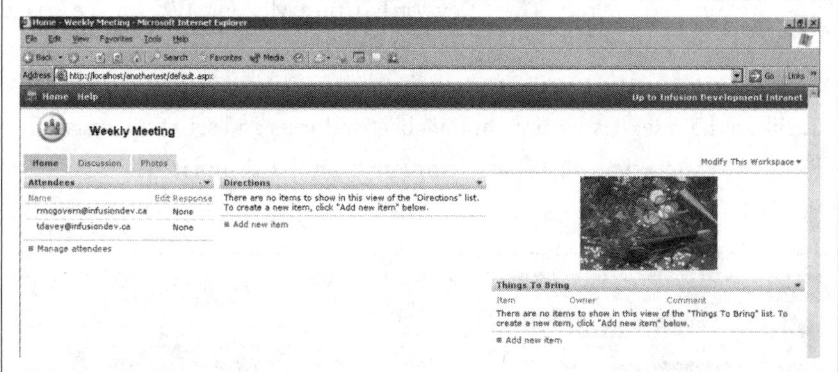

Figure 5-8. Meeting workspace

Blank meeting workspace
: The blank meeting workspace template allows you to create a fully customized meeting workspace.

Decision meeting workspace
: The decision meeting workspace template allows you to review documents and record decisions. The template includes all the lists in the basic meeting template, as well as the document library and tasks and decisions lists.

Social meeting workspace
: The social meeting template is used to plan social events. The template includes a picture library and a discussion board for meeting attendees to post logos and comments. The template also contains the attendees, directions, things to bring, and discussions lists.

Multipage meeting workspace
: The multipage meeting workspace template includes all the functionality of the basic meeting workspace template, but also provides two blank pages to allow you to customize your template.

Creating a meeting workspace through an event

If your existing team site has an existing events list, you can create a meeting workspace site when you add an event:

1. Select the event list on your team site.
2. Click "Add new event."
3. Enter the required information for the event.
4. Select the "Use a Meeting Workspace to organize attendees, agendas, documents, minutes and other details for this event" checkbox.

5. Click Save and Close. The “New or Existing Meeting Workspace” page opens (see Figure 5-9).
6. Select the “Create a new Meeting Workspace” radio button.
7. Fill in the title, description, and web site address and set the permissions.
8. Choose a meeting workspace template from the Template list box.
9. Click OK.

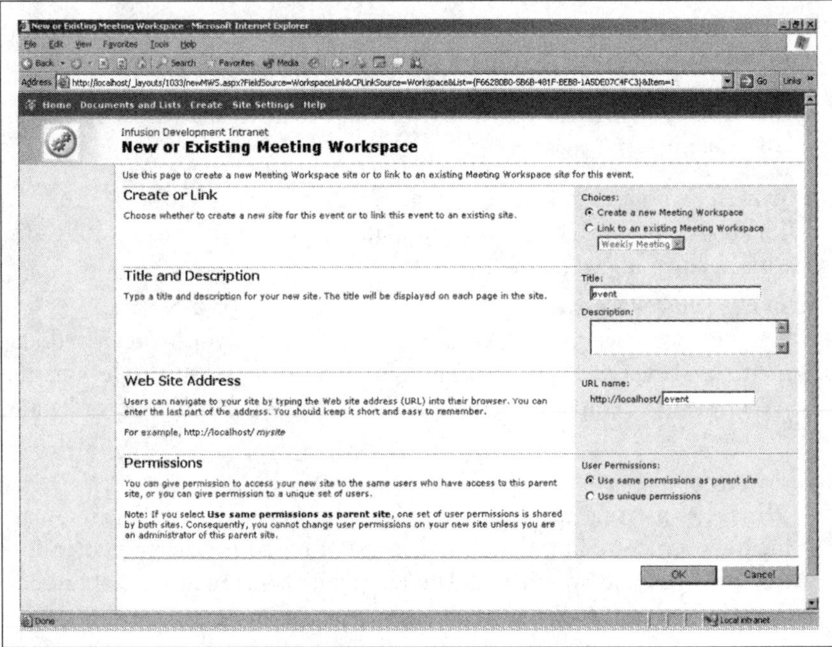

Figure 5-9. New or Existing Meeting Workspace page

Creating a meeting workspace through the Create page

To create a meeting workspace through the Create page without adding an event:

1. Click Create in the top menu bar.
2. Click Sites and Workspaces.
3. Enter a title, description, and web site address and set the permissions.
4. Click Create.
5. Choose the meeting workspace template you want from the Template list box.
6. Click OK.

Meeting workspace Web Parts

Meeting workspaces incorporate the following Web Parts:

Objectives list
: The objective list details the overall purpose of your meeting. Adding an objective list to your meeting workspace lets attendees know what to expect in the meeting and helps all attendees come prepared.

Agenda list
: The agenda list outlines the subjects that will be covered in your meeting, as well as who is responsible for leading the discussions.

Things to bring list
: The things to bring list helps ensure all meeting attendees come to the meeting with the required documents and supplies.

Decisions list
: The decisions list allows users to track any decisions made in your meeting. This feature helps track the progress of any decisions made in your meeting, and to outline the important points of the meeting for users who were unable to attend the meeting.

Attendees list
: The attendees list displays all users who are invited to a meeting. You can also add attendees to the list. If Windows or MSN Messenger is installed, you can implement messaging for all users on the attendees list to invite them to the meeting workspace. Anyone invited to attend the meeting is listed in the attendees list. The attendees list also tracks comments and responses for all meeting attendees. For example, you can reply to a meeting invitation, but note that you will be fifteen minutes late due to a scheduling conflict.

Managing the attendees list

The attendees list should be set up for each new meeting workspace. Figure 5-10 shows the Attendees: New Item page, which is used to add attendees to your meetings. To add an attendee to the attendees list:

1. Navigate to the meeting workspace.
2. Click Documents and Lists in the top menu bar.
3. Click on Meeting Workspace on the side menu.
4. Click on your desired meeting workspace.
5. Click Manage Attendees.
6. Click Add Attendee.

7. If the Address Book feature is available, click on the Address Book button and select the user you want to add to the list.
8. If the Address Book is not available, type in the email address or the username of the person you want to add to the list.

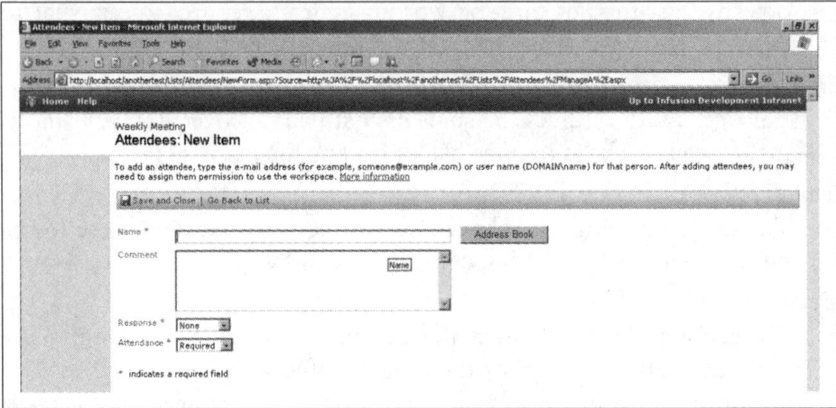

Figure 5-10. Attendees: New Item page

Editing an existing attendee

To edit an existing attendee:

1. Navigate to the meeting workspace.
2. Click Documents and Lists in the top menu bar.
3. Click Meeting Workspace on the side menu.
4. Click on your desired meeting workspace.
5. Click Manage Attendees.
6. Click the Edit icon for the attendee you want to edit.
7. Edit the existing material by changing the name, comment, response, or attendance fields.
8. Click Save and Close.

Deleting an existing attendee

To delete an existing attendee:

1. Navigate to the meeting workspace.
2. Click Documents and Lists in the top menu bar.
3. Click Meeting Workspace on the side menu.

4. Click on your desired meeting workspace.
5. Click Manage Attendees.
6. Select the attendee you want to delete from the attendees list and click the arrow that appears.
7. Select "Delete this item" from the menu.
8. Click OK in the Confirm Delete dialog box.

Form Libraries

SharePoint Services forms are graphical representations of an XML schema that can be used to collect or display data. SharePoint Services integrates with compatible XML editors to allow you to create or import forms to be used on your team site. All SharePoint Services forms are stored in a form library.

Creating a Form Library

A form library provides you with a logical storage location to manage the forms on your SharePoint site. Figure 5-11 shows the New Form Library page, which is used to create new form libraries on your team site. To create a form library:

1. Click Create on the top menu bar.
2. Click Form Library under Document Libraries.
3. Type the form name in the Name text field.
4. Type a brief description of the form in the Description text field. The Description field is optional.
5. If you want your Form Library to appear in the Quick Launch Library, select the Yes radio button in the Navigation section.
6. If you want to create a backup of your form each time it is checked into the form library, select the Yes radio button in the form versions section.
7. Select the form template you want to use for all the forms in the forms library.
8. Click Create.

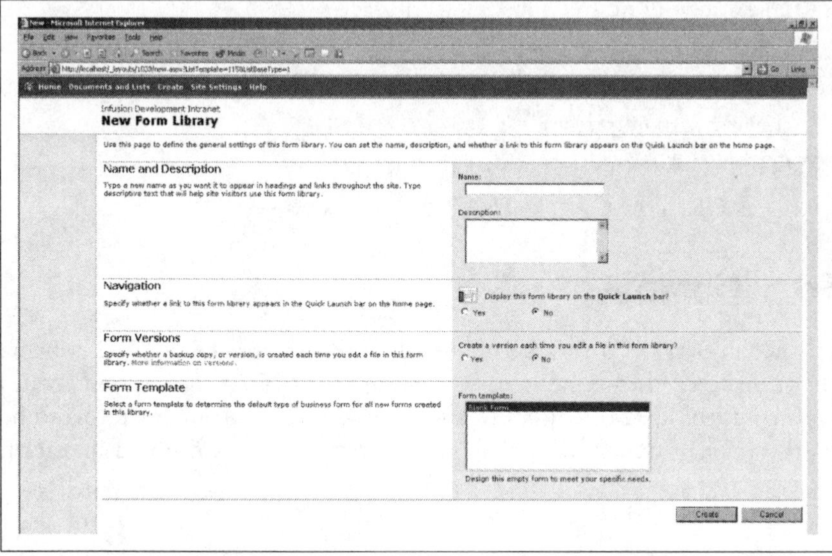

Figure 5-11. Create a new form library

Creating a Blank Form

If there are no form templates available when you create your forms library, by default the form is created as a blank form. To create a blank form template:

1. Click "Modify settings and columns" under the Action section of the page that displays the form library.
2. Click Edit Template in the General Settings sections. To edit the form template, you must have a SharePoint Services–compatible XML editor installed on your computer.

Editing a Form Library's Settings

To change the configuration of a form library:

1. Click Documents and Lists on the top menu bar.
2. Click on the form library you want to open.
3. Click "Modify settings and columns."
4. Click "Change general settings."
5. Edit the existing settings.

Adding a Form to a Form Library

There are two ways to add a form to a form library. You can fill out a blank form that is based on your form template or upload an existing form from your computer.

Filling out a form based on an existing template

To fill out a form based on your form template:

1. Click Documents and Lists on the top menu bar.
2. Click on the form library you want to open.
3. Click Fill Out This Form. After you click the link, the form opens in the program in which the form was created.
4. Fill out the form.
5. Click Save and Close.

Filling out a form based on a blank for template

If you try to fill out a form that uses the blank form template, you will receive an error message because the form doesn't exist yet. You must first create the form using InfoPath. To create a form from the blank form template:

1. Click Documents and Lists on the top menu bar.
2. Click on the myFormLibrary form library.
3. Click Fill Out This Form.

At this point, you will see an error message when InfoPath opens. The form doesn't exist yet, but InfoPath is trying to let you enter data.

To fill out a blank form, you must:

1. Leave InfoPath 2003 open.
2. Select File → Design a Form
3. Click New Blank Form on the righthand menu.
4. Type **`What is your name?`** into the top left of your form.
5. Click Controls.
6. Drag a Text Box and a Button onto your page.
7. Click Save.
8. Click Publish.
9. Click Next.
10. Select the "To a SharePoint form library" radio button.
11. Click Next.

12. Select the "Modify an existing form library" radio button.
13. Click Next.
14. Enter the following URL: **`http://localhost/default.aspx`**.
15. Click Next.
16. Select your form library from the drop-down list.
17. Click Next.
18. Click "Override the existing form template in this form library" radio button.
19. Click Next.
20. Click Finish.
21. Select the "Open this form from its published location" checkbox.
22. Click Close.
23. The form library opens on your Team Site.
24. Click Fill Out This Form.

Uploading an existing form

To upload a form to the form library:

1. Click Documents and Lists on the top menu bar.
2. Click on the form library you want to open.
3. Click Upload Form.
4. Click the Browse button and navigate to the form you want to upload.
5. Click Open.

Editing a Form Template

If the form library is configured to allow you to edit the form template, you can add, delete, or modify form columns directly through a web browser.

To edit a form template:

1. Click Documents and Lists on the top menu bar.
2. Click on the form library you want to open.
3. Click "Modify settings and columns."

Figure 5-12 shows the form library maintenance page. You can edit existing forms, upload and view new forms, or create alerts on the form library maintenance page.

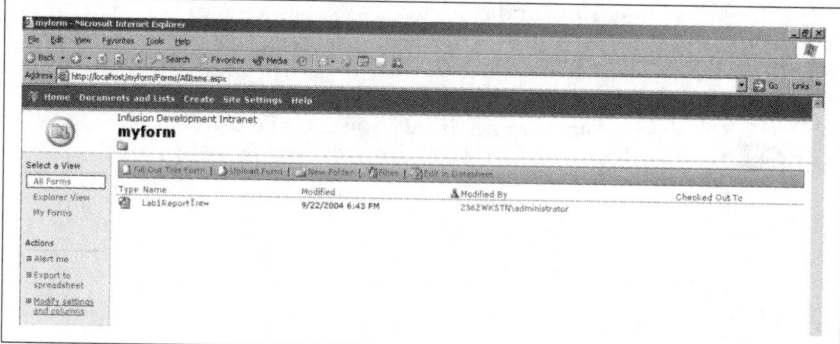

Figure 5-12. Form library maintenance page

Adding a column to a form template

To add a column to a form:

1. Click "Add a new column" in the Columns section.
2. Type a name for the column in the Column name text field.
3. Select the type of information you want the column to display from the Information Type list.
4. Customize the settings of your column.
5. Click OK.

Editing a column on a form

To edit a column on a form:

1. Click on the column you want to edit in the Columns section.
2. Edit the sections you want to change.
3. Click OK.

Deleting a column from a form

To delete a column from a form:

1. Click on the column you want to delete in the Columns section.
2. Click Delete.

Deleting a Form Library

To delete a form library from your SharePoint Services Team site:

1. Click Documents and Lists on the top menu bar.
2. Click on the form library you want to delete.

3. Click “Modify settings and columns.”
4. Click “Delete this form library.”

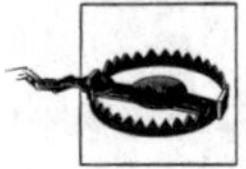

Once a form library is deleted, you cannot recover any of the form library’s contents.

CHAPTER 6

Setting Up Windows SharePoint Services

Whether you are a user or an administrator, you should understand how Windows SharePoint Services is installed and configured. Microsoft has simplified the installation process, allowing you to choose your installation mode and walk away from the server while the installation progresses. Once SharePoint is installed, you can access many configuration options to fine-tune your installation.

In this chapter, you will learn about the options for installing and configuring Windows SharePoint Services. However, detailed installation instructions are beyond the scope of this book. This chapter does provide a high-level overview of the important aspects of the installation process, including:

- Software and hardware requirements
- The process of installing Windows SharePoint Services
- The process for integrating Windows SharePoint Services with SharePoint Portal Server 2003

Once you have read this chapter, you should understand the choices involved in deploying Windows SharePoint Services and be aware of the various configuration options.

Requirements

To use Windows SharePoint Services, you will need a server that meets the minimum requirements. Table 6-1 outlines the hardware, software, and client requirements to run Windows SharePoint Services. Keep in mind that these are only minimum requirements, and most applications require more processing power, memory, and hard disk space.

Table 6-1. Minimum hardware and software requirements for SharePoint Services

Component	Description
Hardware requirements	• Intel Pentium III–compatible processor • 512 MB RAM • 550 MB of free disk space
Software requirements	• One of the following operating systems: —Windows Server 2003, Standard Edition —Windows Server 2003, Enterprise Edition —Windows Server 2003, Datacenter Edition —Windows Server 2003, Web Edition (requires a full version of SQL Server 2000) • Microsoft ASP.NET 1.0 or greater (installed as part of the .NET Framework) • Internet Information Services (IIS) 6.0, containing the following add-ins: —Common Files —Simple Mail Transfer Protocol (SMTP) service —World Wide Web Publishing Service • One of the following versions of SQL Server 2000: —SQL Server 2000, with the latest service pack —SQL Server 2000 Enterprise Edition, with the latest service pack —SQL Server 2000 Desktop Engine (MSDE 2000) —SQL Server 2000 Desktop Engine for Windows (WMSDE)
Client requirements	• One of the following web browsers: —Internet Explorer 5.01 with Service Pack (SP) 2 —Internet Explorer 5.5 with SP 2 —Internet Explorer 6.0 —Netscape Navigator 6.2 or later —Mozilla 1.4 or later

If you have not used or installed Windows 2003 before, it is highly advisable to read up on the technology. Microsoft made many changes to the Windows 2003 installation and configuration process. Most notably, IIS is not installed by default with Windows Server 2003, but it is required for Windows SharePoint Services.

Installing Windows SharePoint Services

Installation of Windows SharePoint Services is done by means of a simple wizard. In most cases, you can follow the defaults, walk away from the server, and the installation will be complete. Instead of going over the installation instructions step by step for Windows SharePoint Services, this chapter looks at the installation from a high-level overview. The topics covered include:

- Deployment options
- Installation process
- Configuring Windows SharePoint Services

Deployment Options

You can install Windows SharePoint Services 2.0 in several different configurations based on the number of servers you wish to use. Each option has different strengths and physical requirements. The option you choose depends on your business requirements and the size of your organization.

Single server

You can deploy an entire SharePoint Services instance to a single server. All SharePoint sites are hosted on this server, as is the database. This option is the quickest and easiest deployment method, but it is also the most limited in terms of scalability and performance.

Although the single-server installation is quick and can simultaneously support many SharePoint sites, it is not recommended for large installations or enterprise organizations. Because both the application server and database server reside within one machine, the server's performance can quickly degrade as more sites are added and more users access the existing sites.

Single-server deployment is recommended for organizations that:

- Expect fewer than 1,000 sites to be hosted.
- Expect a limited number of simultaneous users. The exact number is a function of the machine specifications.
- Want to set up a test site for SharePoint without the overhead of multiple servers.

Even with the potential for performance issues, there are still good reasons for deploying Windows SharePoint Services in a single-server environment. The benefits to using a single server for deployment are:

- The database doesn't require any special configuration. A default installation of Windows SharePoint Services automatically installs WMSDE, which can support most sites.
- You can install Windows SharePoint Services and create and publish a SharePoint web site based on the WMSDE database in minutes.

- Several SharePoint web sites can be hosted with minimal overhead.
- By modifying the installation, Windows SharePoint Services can use SQL Server 2000 Enterprise or Standard Edition as the database. This allows for more SharePoint web sites.

Figure 6-1 illustrates how a client interacts with a single-server SharePoint installation.

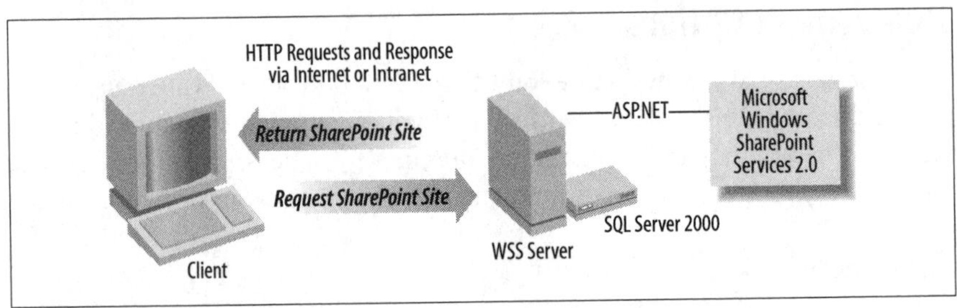

Figure 6-1. Single-server deployment

Note that the database, the web server, and the SharePoint sites are all stored on a single server. Multiple clients can access the server via HTTP.

Remote SQL Server

Using Windows SharePoint Services on a single server satisfies most small-to medium-sized businesses. However, if you plan to run Windows SharePoint Services in an enterprise environment, or where more than 1,000 SharePoint sites will be hosted, Microsoft highly advises you to separate SQL Server from SharePoint.

By placing SQL Server on a separate machine, you gain the following benefits:

- The server hosting Windows SharePoint Services can devote its processor, disk resources, and memory to providing SharePoint sites and files.
- The server hosting SQL Server can devote its processor, disk resources, and memory to database management.
- An increase in performance and sites served to clients.

Deploying with a remote SQL Server creates an assembly-line scenario. The client asks the web server for a SharePoint page. The web server requests any necessary data from the database. Upon receipt of the information from the database server, the web server generates and returns the SharePoint page to the client. Each server performs a specialized task and can be optimized for that task. Figure 6-2 illustrates how a remote SQL Server deployment interacts with a client.

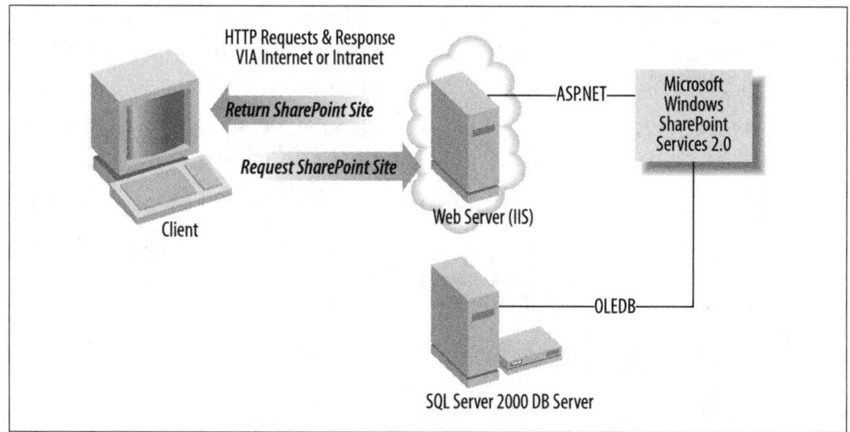

Figure 6-2. Remote SQL Server deployment

Note that the web server hosts IIS, Windows SharePoint Services, and any SharePoint sites. The database server hosts SQL Server. By separating the functionality, you can customize each server for its specific role. You might, for example, use a storage area network for the database server, or tune the connections on the web server to support more clients.

Server farm

Unfortunately, separating the database onto a separate server from the application will not solve all the performance concerns of an organization. Eventually, either your database server or application server (or both) will begin to run low on resources. Once this occurs, performance will begin to degrade. Fortunately, Windows SharePoint Services can also be deployed in a fully scalable server-farm configuration.

A server farm allows you to load balance your Windows SharePoint Services installation to provide maximum efficiency and performance. With a server farm, you can add additional servers (both application and database) to balance the load of the application.

In Windows SharePoint Services, a server farm will have the following characteristics:

- Multiple servers are running Windows SharePoint Services and SQL Server.
- Sites and subsites are grouped into site collection. Each site collection exists within a virtual server in IIS and uses an ISAPI filter to map incoming URLs to specific sites on each virtual server.
- Each virtual server has its own set of databases within SQL Server.

- For each additional web server added, a higher throughput of content is achieved and more content can be displayed by the Windows SharePoint Services.
- To balance the load that is incurred across all servers, special switching and routing hardware or software can be used for load balancing.

Figure 6-3 demonstrates how a server farm interacts with a client.

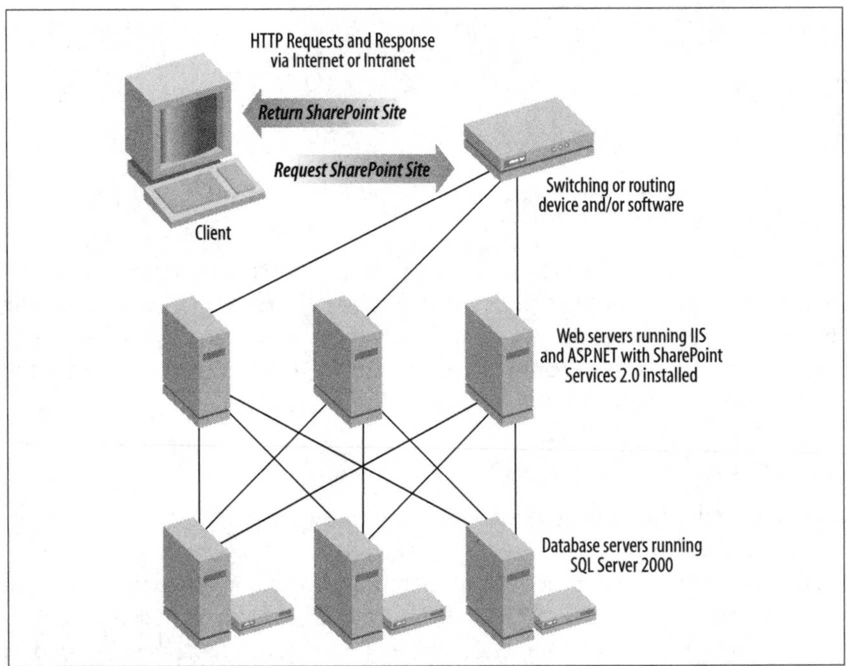

Figure 6-3. Server farm deployment

The exact details of a server farm depend on your available equipment and needs. For example, the switching and routing functionality may be performed by dedicated hardware or software such as the built-in Windows 2003 clustering and load-balancing systems.

Installation Process

Once you have chosen your deployment configuration, you are ready to install Windows SharePoint Services. The deployment mode you select determines the configuration options you need to choose during the installation process. Fortunately, many of the configurations you select during installation can be modified after the installation through the SharePoint Central Administration site.

Considerations prior to installation

Even though many of the configuration options you select during the installation can be modified, you need to make sure you understand the choices before installing the software. Post-installation changes can severely disrupt the uptime of Windows SharePoint Services, thus affecting the users who are attempting to access it. Further, there are some options that cannot be modified after the installation without a full uninstall and reinstall of Windows SharePoint Services.

The following is a list of configuration options that should be analyzed prior to beginning an installation of Windows SharePoint Services:

- User account mode
- Database type
- IIS application pool
- FrontPage 2002 Server Extensions

User account mode. There are two types of user account modes that can be selected during the installation:

Domain Account mode
: Grants users access to the site by using their existing Microsoft Windows Domain accounts.

Active Directory Account Creation mode
: Grants users access to the site through Active Directory accounts. If you are using this mode, you must create the user accounts in Active Directory and allow those accounts within Active Directory to have access to Windows SharePoint Services.

Once one of the two options has been selected, you cannot change it. Nor can you run both modes at the same time.

For more information on the impact of choosing an account mode, see the section "Users and Site Groups" in Chapter 4.

Database type. During the installation, you can choose whether you want to install Windows SharePoint Services using an MSDE version of SQL Server or using a full installation version of SQL Server. Unlike the account mode option, you are not stuck with your choice once it is selected. At any time you can change from MSDE to SQL Server.

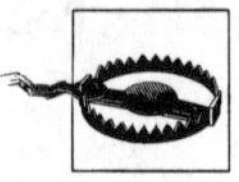

While technically it is possible to move from SQL Server back to MSDE, it is not recommended. MSDE has fewer features than SQL Server, and you will lose functionality if you attempt to move your database from SQL Server to MSDE.

If you choose to install SQL Server, you must also select a database authentication mode:

- Windows Integrated authentication
- SQL Server authentication

If you have worked with SQL Server previously, you will be familiar with these two options. Windows authentication does not transmit usernames or passwords between servers. Rather, it relies on the IIS application pool to handle domain credential verification. Integrated authentication improves SQL Server security because you are relying on secure transmission of credentials. You can also take advantage of the Windows user management system to create new accounts.

Conversely, SQL Server authentication transmits usernames and passwords between servers in an unencrypted form. This creates a much less secure environment. In addition, the SQL Server administrator must create and maintain all necessary user accounts.

One other important note is that you do not need to install either SQL Server or MSDE if you already have a copy installed on your target server. If this is the case, you can simply attach Windows SharePoint Services to the previously installed copy of SQL Server. You will often use this option when you are deploying to a distributed environment where SQL Server is on a separate computer (or cluster).

IIS application pool. Application pools are an IIS 6.0 feature that permits separate, isolated processes to run your web applications. Because each application pool will have a unique identity, you can identify which web application is executing actions based on the application pool identity.

In previous versions of IIS (before 6.0), all web applications were run inside the IIS process. If IIS crashed, all your web applications also crashed. To mitigate this risk, IIS 6.0 assigns web applications to specific application pools, creating virtual sandboxes. Now, if one application pool crashes, the remaining application pools will continue to function as though nothing happened.

With regards to Windows SharePoint Services, you can configure the application pool during installation by choosing one of four options:

- The administrative virtual server uses one application pool, but a separate pool is used for other sites.
- All virtual servers share an application pool.
- Each virtual server receives its own application pool.
- Virtual servers that host the same web sites share an application pool.

If SharePoint is deployed in a server-farm mode, or you expect to create multiple virtual servers, you will probably want to use either the third or fourth option, as these options will prevent SharePoint from stopping completely if one of the application pools crashes.

FrontPage 2002 Server Extensions. If installed, FrontPage 2002 Server Extensions are generally found using port 80. This will cause a conflict with Windows SharePoint Services. If you find that FrontPage 2002 Server Extensions are running on port 80, back up your virtual server and, using Microsoft SharePoint Administrator, unextend the virtual server. After the installation of Windows SharePoint Services, you can restore your FrontPage 2002 Server Extensions to a different virtual server running on another port or to the same virtual server and upgrade the extensions to Windows SharePoint Services.

Installing Windows SharePoint Services

Once you've considered your choices and made all the important decisions each choice entails, you can now install Windows SharePoint Services. Installing SharePoint is very similar to any other Microsoft installation. There are two types of installation modes:

Typical
: This will install Windows SharePoint Services and set up the IIS default virtual server to be a SharePoint team site. It will also install WMSDE (MSDE for Windows) as the default database.

Server farm
: This will install only Windows SharePoint Services. The database and IIS configurations must be made after the installation is complete.

There is a third installation method known as a *quiet installation*. Under a quiet installation, no user intervention is required. The user will never be prompted to supply any information or see any messages. A quiet installation needs to be run from the command line using the *setupsts.exe* installer and specifying the `/q` command to indicate that you want to run the installation in quiet mode. A quiet installation can be configured to perform either a typical or server-farm style installation.

Extending virtual servers

When you install IIS, a default virtual server running on port 80 (HTTP default) is created for you. This virtual server hosts all your SharePoint sites on your server, and allows others to connect through it to view your sites. A single IIS installation can have multiple virtual severs configured; however, each server typically runs on its own port.

Windows SharePoint Services uses virtual servers to host its sites. Windows SharePoint Services attaches to a virtual server to create this link. The attachment process is referred to as *extending* a server and is used for other applications such as Microsoft FrontPage Server Extensions.

Before you can create any SharePoint sites, you must extend at least one virtual server. When installing SharePoint in a single-server environment, SharePoint will automatically extend the virtual server on the local computer and create a default site for you. However, if you are installing SharePoint in a complicated environment, such as a server farm, you will have to manually extend each virtual server separately.

Configuring Windows SharePoint Services

After Windows SharePoint Services has been installed, you have multiple configuration options to help you fine-tune your system. You can manage these options using the SharePoint Central Administration site, which is automatically deployed with your installation. Through this site, you can configure the following:

- The virtual server
- Security for SharePoint
- The server
- Components that SharePoint uses

With any Windows SharePoint installation, the Central Administration site is accesible through the Administrative Tools section in Windows Server 2003. Figure 6-4 shows the Central Administration site and the administration options available.

The central administration site is divided into several different configuration sections. See the section "Security Architecture" in Chapter 4.

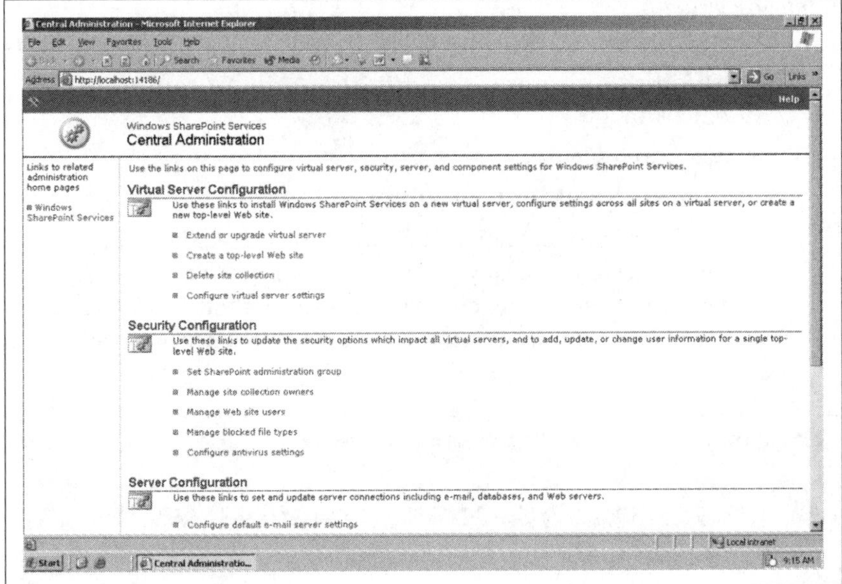

Figure 6-4. SharePoint Central Administration site

Virtual server configuration

The virtual server controls access to SharePoint team sites. Configuring the virtual server allows you to manage the following options:

Extend or upgrade virtual server
: This option allows you to manage your virtual servers, create new content databases, and extend your virtual server to map to another virtual server. You will need to access this option if you have not extended a virtual server. For instance, if you selected server farm as your installation option, you will need to extend each of the servers in the farm.

Create a top-level web site
: By default, a top-level web site is created for you when you perform a typical installation. However, if one does not exist, or you need to create another top-level web site, you can use this option. From this screen, you can assign the site owners, select a quota template, and choose the site language.

Delete site collection
: At any time, you can remove a top-level web site. By using this option, you can delete an entire top-level web site, including all subsites that exist within it.

Configure virtual server settings

SharePoint, when installed through a typical installation, creates three virtual servers:

- Administration
- Default web site
- Microsoft SharePoint Administration

The virtual server configuration allows you to manage the settings for all three virtual servers and any other virtual servers that you may have extended for use with SharePoint. Figure 6-5 shows the Virtual Server Settings page. The majority of your site administration exists within this area.

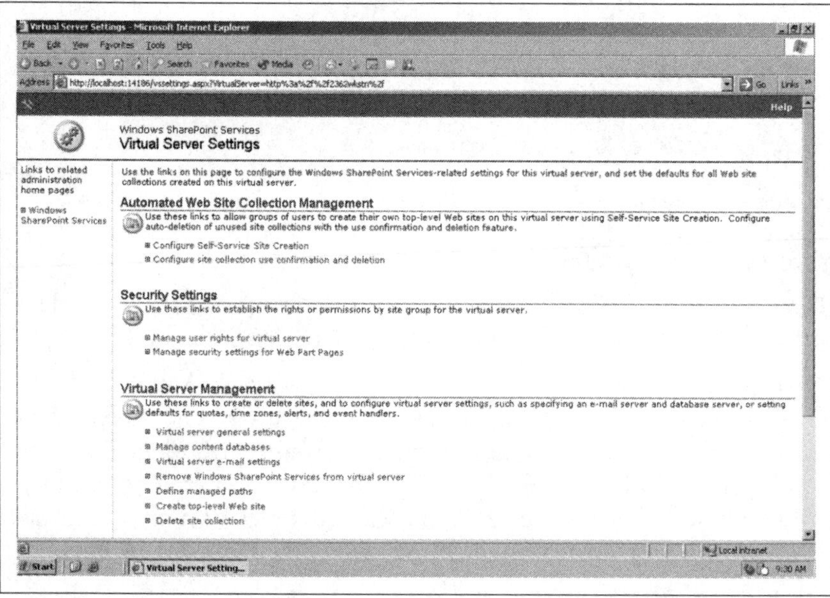

Figure 6-5. Virtual Server Settings

From the Virtual Server Settings screen, you can:

Automate web site collection management

Enables users to create top-level web sites on the virtual server. You can also configure site collections to be autodeleted if they are not in use.

Set security for the virtual server and Web Part pages

Enables you to manage rights and permissions for site groups and users.

Configure the virtual server

Enables you to change the general settings for the virtual server.

Manage content databases
: Enables you to change the content databases for the virtual server.

Establish email settings
: Enables you to configure the email server and settings.

Remove Windows SharePoint Services from the virtual server
: Enables you to remove Windows SharePoint Services from the virtual server.

Define managed paths
: Enables you to specify the paths in the virtual server that Windows SharePoint Services will manage.

Create a top-level web site
: Enables you to create a new top-level web site.

Delete a site collection
: Enables you to remove a site collection from the virtual server.

Configure components
: Enables you to configure the data-retrieval service settings.

Security configuration

With the use of both Active Directory and Windows NT User Accounts, Windows SharePoint Services has made a strong attempt to lessen the burden on administering user accounts. Configuring security allows you to manage the following options:

Set SharePoint administration group
: By selecting this option, you grant a Windows NT group administrative access. By default, the administrator user account is given administrative access to SharePoint. Similarly, the owner of any team site is automatically granted administrative access over that specific site. However, if you want to grant administrative control to a group of users, you can grant global administrative access to a Windows NT group account.

Manage site collection owners
: Whenever you create a new team site in SharePoint, you must specify a site owner. This option allows you to change who the owner is after the site has been created.

Manage web site users
: You can grant users specific roles to any of the SharePoint team sites. By using this screen, you can add, modify, and delete roles for a user to a specific team site.

Manage blocked file types
: In order to prevent malicious files from being uploaded or to stop users from downloading files that they should not be downloading, you can block file types. This screen allows you to prevent specific file types from being saved or downloaded from SharePoint.

Configure antivirus settings
: Because SharePoint allows users to upload and download files from SharePoint team sites, you will want to protect your servers and users' machines from receiving a virus. This screen allows you to configure settings to scan documents when users upload documents to or download documents from the virtual server.

Virus scanning software must be present on all web servers before these settings will work.

Server configuration

After installing Windows SharePoint Services, there are several server-based options that are not turned on or set up by default. To modify these settings, use the following options:

Manage email server settings
: In order to use certain SharePoint functionality (such as alerts), you must configure the email options. From this screen, you can identify an SMTP server and specify the From and Reply-to email addresses to be used when sending email from a SharePoint site.

Manage the web server list
: When you are running a server farm, you will want to control what your servers are doing. From this screen, you can not only manage all the servers in your server farm, but also remove servers from your farm.

Manage the database server
: There are two options that can be performed in this section:

- Set default content database server
- Set configuration database server

The first option allows you to specify the location of your database server. A default single-server installation shows your local server name. The second option allows you to decide how to connect to the database.

Configure the HTML Viewer
: SharePoint allows you to configure an HTML Viewer service. The HTML Viewer service will automatically translate Microsoft Office document

types such as PowerPoint and Word into standard HTML. In other words, by configuring the HTML Viewer, you can allow users to view Microsoft Office documents (e.g., *.doc*, *.xls*, *.ppt*) without the required software. From this screen, you can enable this service and point SharePoint to the location of the translation program(s).

Configure the virtual server for central administration
: As mentioned previously, application pools are used to host SharePoint sites. From this screen, you can connect the SharePoint Central Administration site to an existing application pool, or generate a new application pool to support the administration site. Generally, you will want to have the administration site running under a different application pool than ordinary user sites. That way, if the user sites are malfunctioning, you should still be able to access the administrative site to analyze the problem and make any repairs.

Component configuration

There are some global components that can be configured after the installation. These components are used across all SharePoint sites. To configure components, you can use the following options:

Manage full-text searching
: Full-text searching is a feature that is only available if you are using SQL Server 2000 Standard or Enterprise Edition. If you are using a full version of SQL Server, you can use this option to enable and disable full-text searching.

Manage the usage analysis processing
: Usage analysis allows you to monitor all your SharePoint team sites. This information can provide you with a strong idea of how users are accessing and using SharePoint sites. This option lets you set up the logging and processing of data for usage analysis.

Manage quotas and locks
: In smaller installations, site quotas and locks are not a major concern. However, when dealing with larger implementations of SharePoint, you will want to limit how many resources are allocated to different sites. This section allows you to set limits on data storage and the number of users allowed for a site collection.

Manage the data-retrieval service settings
: Using SOAP and XML, this new type of data-retrieval service allows data to be sent and received from different data sources. This option allows you to enable data-retrieval services, limit the response size of SOAP messages, enable update query support, and set the timeout for the data source.

Integrating with SharePoint Portal Server 2003

Windows SharePoint Services provides a powerful suite of functions for developing portals and working collaboratively. However, Windows SharePoint Services only provides part of the total information portal solution.

SharePoint Portal Server

SharePoint Portal Server 2003 extends Windows SharePoint Services by adding many new features to assist larger and more robust collaborative work environments. In particular, SharePoint Portal Server 2003 provides a solution that enables enterprises to:

- Use single sign-on to enable easy access and relieve administrators from having to maintain multiple user data stores
- Integrate information from various systems (such as Microsoft BizTalk 2004) into a single coherent portal
- Employ a complete end-to-end solution that allows users to search for people, teams, and information through audiences, automatic categorization, site directories, and user profiles
- Use new deployment and management tools to meet the ever-changing needs of the corporate enterprises

The Relationship Between Windows SharePoint Services and SharePoint Portal Server 2003

Although SharePoint Portal Server 2003 provides more features than Windows SharePoint Services, it is very important to remember that SharePoint Portal Server 2003 is an extension of Windows SharePoint Services. Whereas Windows SharePoint Services allows you to create sites for team collaboration, SharePoint Portal Server 2003 connects these sites to create a global directory. In other words, SharePoint Portal provides a unified interface into all team sites.

Another thing to keep in mind is that many of the features in SharePoint Portal Server 2003 require Windows SharePoint Services. For instance, user profiles are built by using Web Parts, which is a feature from Windows SharePoint Services. In other words, Windows SharePoint Services and SharePoint Portal Server 2003 work together to provide a single, complete portal solution. Figure 6-6 illustrates the relationship between SharePoint Portal Server and SharePoint Services.

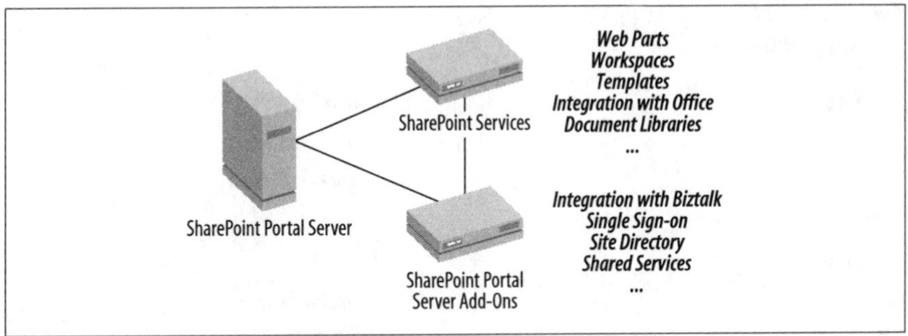

Figure 6-6. SharePoint relationships

Comparing features of Windows SharePoint Services and SharePoint Portal Server 2003

Table 6-2 provides a feature list of many of the items in SharePoint Portal Server. This table identifies whether the feature is exclusive to SharePoint Portal Server 2003 or if the feature also exists in Windows SharePoint Services. Because SharePoint Portal Server 2003 requires Windows SharePoint Services, none of the features of Windows SharePoint Services are excluded from SharePoint Portal Server.

Table 6-2. Feature matrix of SharePoint Server and Windows SharePoint Services

Feature	Both/SharePoint Portal Server
Alerts	Both
Automatic categorization	SharePoint Portal Server
Audiences	SharePoint Portal Server
Customization from the browser	Both
Discussion boards	Both
Document libraries	Both
Document workspaces	Both
Integration with Biztalk	SharePoint Portal Server
Integration with Microsoft FrontPage 2003	Both
Integration with Microsoft InfoPath 2003	Both
Integration with Microsoft Office 2003	Both
Lists	Both
Meetings	Both
News	SharePoint Portal Server
Personal sites	SharePoint Portal Server
Shared services	SharePoint Portal Server

Table 6-2. Feature matrix of SharePoint Server and Windows SharePoint Services (continued)

Feature	Both/SharePoint Portal Server
Single sign-on	SharePoint Portal Server
Site directory	SharePoint Portal Server
Surveys	Both
Templates	Both
Topic areas	SharePoint Portal Server
User profiles	SharePoint Portal Server
Web Part pages	Both

Choosing SharePoint Portal Server or Windows SharePoint Services

If SharePoint Portal Server 2003 is an extension of Windows SharePoint Services, when should one be chosen over the other? Table 6-3 provides some guidance for common enterprise scenarios.

Table 6-3. SharePoint Portal Server 2003 versus Windows SharePoint Services

Business problem	Solution
Sharing documents with team members	Windows SharePoint Services. While SharePoint Portal Server 2003 contains Document libraries, if this is the main problem you are trying to solve, Windows SharePoint Services will more than suffice.
Integrating data from several applications into a central location	SharePoint Portal Server. By including the integration of Microsoft Biztalk Server, you can easily accomplish this task.
Sharing contact lists, events, and announcements	Windows SharePoint Services. Windows SharePoint Services allows you to use team sites to post contacts, events, and announcements.
Providing users with easy login options and centralizing the location of user accounts	SharePoint Portal Server. Single sign-on allows users to log in using their Microsoft Windows NT user accounts. Administrators do not have to create additional accounts for users, nor do users have to remember additional passwords.
Allowing users to create their own sites	Windows SharePoint Services. By turning on Self Service Site Creation, users can quickly create their own sites. This frees administrators from having to create sites for the users on demand.
Targeting content based on user roles or interests	SharePoint Portal Server. Using the Audiences feature in SharePoint Portal Server, you can target Web Parts, news, lists, and list items to different audiences.
Notification on document changes	Windows SharePoint Services. By using alerts, users can find out whenever a document has changed.
Managing multiple SharePoint sites	SharePoint Portal Server. You can add, modify, and delete multiple SharePoint sites from SharePoint Portal Server.

Keep in mind that Windows SharePoint Services is the simpler solution; however, SharePoint Portal Server provides additional features. If you choose to use SharePoint Portal Server, you gain all of Windows SharePoint Services, plus the additional features.

Integrating Windows SharePoint Services with SharePoint Portal Server

Even though SharePoint Portal Server 2003 extends Windows SharePoint Services, integration between the two applications is not completely seamless. As with any upgrade (or in this case, integration), it is advisable to back up the server prior to beginning the integration.

Prior to installing SharePoint Portal Server 2003, there are two tasks that need to be completed:

- Verify the configuration is supported.
- Record the SQL Server database names.

Once you have completed these tasks, you can proceed to install and configure SharePoint Portal Server.

Verify configuration

Two Windows SharePoint Services configurations are not supported during an install by SharePoint Portal Server:

- Scalable Hosting mode
- Active Directory Account Creation mode

Unfortunately, if either of these modes has been installed, you cannot install SharePoint Portal Server 2003 over Windows SharePoint Services. These options are set during the installation of Windows SharePoint Services and cannot be changed.

To find out if you are in Scalable Hosting mode, open the configuration database for Windows SharePoint Services. Find the Globals table and open it. Search for the UseHostHeader column. If the value is `1` in UseHostHeader, you are in Scalable Hosting mode.

To determine if you are using Active Directory Account Creation mode, open the SharePoint Central Administration site. If the options to create a top-level site, enable Self-Service Site Creation, and adding users are not available, you are in Active Directory account mode.

In either case, you will not be able to integrate your existing Windows SharePoint Service installation with a new installation of SharePoint Portal Server.

Record SQL Server database names

During the installation of SharePoint Portal Server 2003, one of the steps will be to identify your database. If you specify the settings of the current Windows SharePoint Services installation, all of the functionality from your existing virtual servers will be retained. Otherwise, your new SharePoint Portal Server 2003 will be created with no information pertaining to the existing Windows SharePoint Services sites.

You can use the SharePoint Central Administration site to gather the names and settings of your content databases for use in the SharePoint Portal Server installation. Figure 6-7 shows the Set Configuration Database Server screen that allows you to enter the configuration information for your databases.

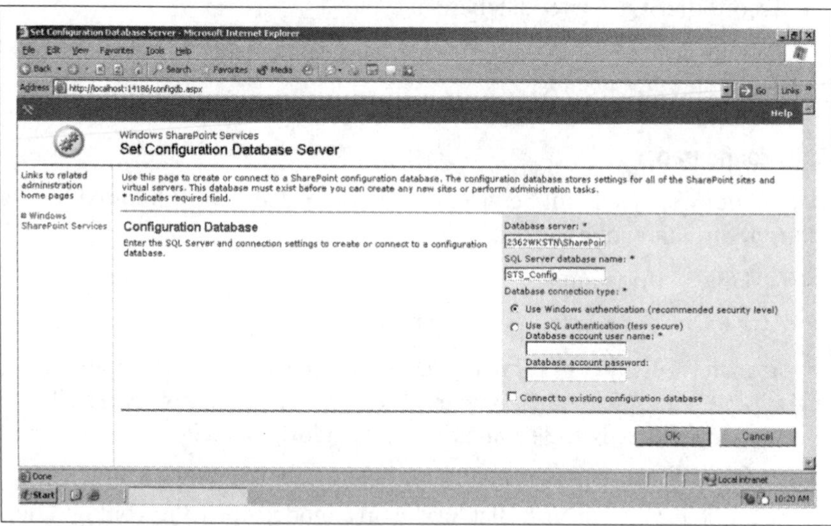

Figure 6-7. Database configuration information

You should note all of the details for each database in your current installation before beginning the installation of SharePoint Portal Server.

Install and configure SharePoint Portal Server 2003

For the most part, installing and configuring SharePoint Portal Server 2003 over an existing Windows SharePoint Services installation is very straightforward. However, as with all things, there are some important items to note:

- All virtual servers and content databases will be stopped and disconnected during the installation. You have to manually reconnect the virtual servers to SharePoint Portal Server 2003 once the installation is complete.
- In a server farm, you must install SharePoint Portal Server 2003 on every server that contains an instance of Windows SharePoint Services.
- If the virtual servers for both Windows SharePoint Services and SharePoint Portal Server 2003 are located on the same machine and use the same port, you must apply host headers to allow for navigation to the correct sites.
- You must create a new virtual server in SharePoint Portal Server 2003 and extend it to map to your existing Windows SharePoint Services virtual servers to access existing SharePoint sites.

Consider the Microsoft SharePoint Migration Tool

As mentioned previously, you need to create a new virtual server once SharePoint Portal Server 2003 has been installed over Windows SharePoint Services. By configuring the new virtual server to extend the existing Windows SharePoint Services virtual servers, you can now access your existing SharePoint team sites. Fortunately, there is another way to map to your existing SharePoint team sites without having to create a new virtual server manually.

The Microsoft SharePoint Migration Tool (*smigrate.exe*) provides you with a method of moving your existing Windows SharePoint Services sites to SharePoint Portal Server 2003. The Migration Tool:

- Backs up all sites to a file
- Restores the sites to the new location

If you have many sites, or the site you are trying to migrate is large, this process could take a very long time to complete. In order to increase performance, you should configure the process with:

- One server running the Migration Tool
- One or more servers acting as the web servers
- One or more servers acting as the database servers

Once you have completed migration, you should be able to leverage the full features of SharePoint Portal Server.

Windows SharePoint Services Service Pack 1

Microsoft released the first service pack for Windows SharePoint Services on September 2, 2004. The service pack contains important security enhancements and fixes issues not covered in a Microsoft Knowledge Based article previously released. Service pack 1 fixes the following issues:

- A "Bad Request" error message is displayed when entering **`//localhost`** in Internet Explorer.
- A Web Part not being added to the online Web Part gallery.
- Restoring a SQL database causes links at the root of a web site to break.
- Relinking a form in SharePoint Services causes formatted text to move.
- Oldest items in threaded view in a discussion are listed first.
- Backing up SharePoint Services causes a "Write error" error message.
- An "Error 403.1" error message is displayed when you create a new SharePoint web site.
- Installing a language SharePoint template pack does not add the language to the Select Language list.
- A "Form Validation Error" error message is displayed when uploading a large file.
- A nonprovisioned web site is provisioned when installing or updating a SharePoint server.
- If you update SharePoint, IIS services that were originally stopped may be restarted automatically.
- Opening a SharePoint web page causes FrontPage to quit.
- Installing an update that contains the *Mso.dll* file may cause Microsoft Office programs to indicate an incorrect service pack level.
- Some SharePoint files have certificate expiration dates that are earlier than expected.
- Adding a user through Microsoft Windows groups corrupts the UserInfo field on the home page.
- Multiple threads accessing the same document at the same time on SharePoint causes an "Access Violation" error message.

- Entering **`//localhost`** in Internet Explorer on a Windows Server 2003 machine causes a "Not authorized" error message to be displayed.
- Pasting text in a new announcement that contains extended characters fails.
- If the file properties contain a nonbreaking space, it will corrupt the XML file in SharePoint.

Index

We'd like to hear your suggestions for improving our indexes. Send email to *index@oreilly.com*.

E

F

H

I

L

M

N

O

P

Q

S

T

U

V

W

X

About the Authors

On Wall Street and in City Hall, billions of dollars flow annually through systems developed by **Infusion Development Corporation**. Infusion is the trusted development partner of some of the world's largest investment banks as well as a number of the largest state agencies in the United States. As a proven leader in the design and implementation of enterprise-scale financial systems and strategic portals, Infusion has built a reputation as the "go-to shop" for many of the world's largest and most sophisticated enterprises. For information on training services, mentoring, strategic consulting, and on/off-site implementation, visit *http://www.infusiondev.com*.

Bryan Acker is Technical Writer at Infusion Development Canada in Toronto. He has developed ASP and ASP.NET web applications for financial and medical institutions in the Pittsburgh area. He has worked with Microsoft technology for several years, writing MSDN whitepapers for ASP.NET 2.0 as well as developing courseware for several of Infusion's training engagements.

Bryan, an avid surfer, is also a published fiction author and contributes to several local music web sites in the Toronto area.

Tyler Davey is a developer and writer at Infusion Development Canada in Toronto. Tyler has developed products for the U.S. military, major banking institutions, and automotive suppliers. Tyler has a wife and two Jack Russell terriers and tries to balance his free time between his family, coaching hockey, and writing.

Robert McGovern works as a consultant, architect, project manager, and trainer for Infusion Development Corporation. He has worked on everything from large mortgage and stock-trading systems to biomechanics data collection and analysis systems. Rob currently lives in Colorado with his wife and daughter.

Rob is the author of several technology books covering everything from development languages to databases. Rob has also authored several articles on MSDN and other developer-oriented web sites.

Colophon

Our look is the result of reader comments, our own experimentation, and feedback from distribution channels. Distinctive covers complement our distinctive approach to technical topics, breathing personality and life into potentially dry subjects.

The animals on the cover of *SharePoint User's Guide* are a rooster and hens (*Gallus domesticus*). Roosters (male chickens) and hens (female chickens) are domesticated birds believed to have descended from the wild Asian red junglefowl. They are omnivorous, feeding on small seeds, herbs and leaves, grubs, insects, and even small mammals such as mice. Chickens can fly only short distances but can usually clear a barnyard fence if their feathers are not clipped. Since it is so widespread, the chicken is considered to be the most common bird in the world, with a population count reaching 24 billion (as of 2003).

Humans have benefited enormously from the chicken's efficient reproductive process. When a rooster is placed among a flock of hens, fertile eggs generally appear within a couple of days. When a rooster dies or is removed from the flock, the hens will continue to produce fertile eggs for up to four weeks thanks to their handy "sperm nest" areas, which collect and store semen for later use. Hens quite clearly prefer dominant males to low-ranking ones, and almost always resist copulation with the latter. They try first to run from the assailant before sending out a cry for help to the dominant rooster. If all else fails, the hen simply ejects the assailant's sperm back in his direction immediately after the sexual attack.

Matt Hutchinson was the production editor for *SharePoint User's Guide*. GEX, Inc. provided production services. Lydia Onofrei, Emily Quill, Claire Cloutier, and Colleen Gorman provided quality control.

Ellie Volckhausen designed the cover of this book, based on a series design by Edie Freedman. The cover image is a 19th-century engraving from an unknown source. Emma Colby produced the cover layout with Adobe InDesign CS using Adobe's ITC Garamond font.

David Futato designed the interior layout. This book was converted by Andrew Savikas and Judy Hoer to FrameMaker 5.5.6 with a format conversion tool created by Erik Ray, Jason McIntosh, Neil Walls, and Mike Sierra that uses Perl and XML technologies. The text font is Linotype Birka; the heading font is Adobe Myriad Condensed; and the code font is LucasFont's TheSans Mono Condensed. The illustrations that appear in the book were produced by Robert Romano, Jessamyn Read, and Lesley Borash using Macromedia FreeHand 9 and Adobe Photoshop 6. The tip and warning icons were drawn by Christopher Bing. This colophon was written by Lydia Onofrei.

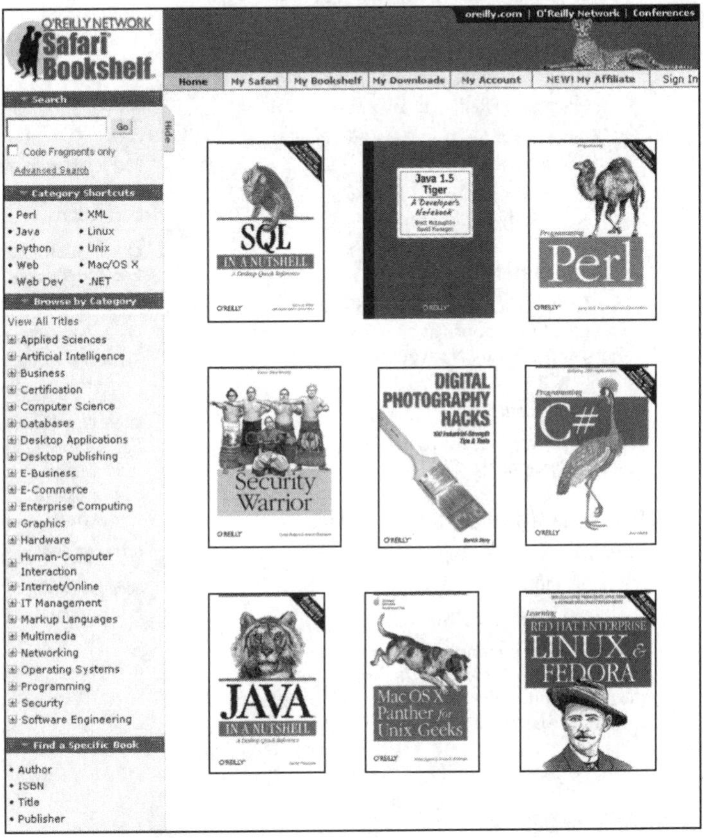

Keep in touch with O'Reilly

1. Download examples from our books

To find example files for a book, go to:

www.oreilly.com/catalog

select the book, and follow the "Examples" link.

2. Register your O'Reilly books

Register your book at *register.oreilly.com*

Why register your books? Once you've registered your O'Reilly books you can:

- Win O'Reilly books, T-shirts or discount coupons in our monthly drawing.
- Get special offers available only to registered O'Reilly customers.
- Get catalogs announcing new books (US and UK only).
- Get email notification of new editions of the O'Reilly books you own.

3. Join our email lists

Sign up to get topic-specific email announcements of new books and conferences, special offers, and O'Reilly Network technology newsletters at:

elists.oreilly.com

It's easy to customize your free elists subscription so you'll get exactly the O'Reilly news you want.

4. Get the latest news, tips, and tools

http://www.oreilly.com

- "Top 100 Sites on the Web"—PC Magazine
- CIO Magazine's Web Business 50 Awards

Our web site contains a library of comprehensive product information (including book excerpts and tables of contents), downloadable software, background articles, interviews with technology leaders, links to relevant sites, book cover art, and more.

5. Work for O'Reilly

Check out our web site for current employment opportunities:

jobs.oreilly.com

6. Contact us

O'Reilly & Associates
1005 Gravenstein Hwy North
Sebastopol, CA 95472 USA

TEL: 707-827-7000 or 800-998-9938
(6am to 5pm PST)

FAX: 707-829-0104

order@oreilly.com
For answers to problems regarding your order or our products.
To place a book order online, visit:

www.oreilly.com/order_new

catalog@oreilly.com
To request a copy of our latest catalog.

booktech@oreilly.com
For book content technical questions or corrections.

corporate@oreilly.com
For educational, library, government, and corporate sales.

proposals@oreilly.com
To submit new book proposals to our editors and product managers.

international@oreilly.com
For information about our international distributors or translation queries. For a list of our distributors outside of North America check out:

international.oreilly.com/distributors.html

adoption@oreilly.com
For information about academic use of O'Reilly books, visit:

academic.oreilly.com